W9-BHX-618

Pocket
BUDAPEST
TOP SIGHTS • LOCAL LIFE • MADE EASY

Steve Fallon

In This Book

QuickStart Guide

Your keys to understanding the city – we help you decide what to do and how to do it

Need to Know
Tips for a smooth trip

Neighbourhoods
What's where

Explore Budapest

The best things to see and do, neighbourhood by neighbourhood

Top Sights
Make the most of your visit

Local Life
The insider's city

The Best of Budapest

The city's highlights in handy lists to help you plan

Best Walks
See the city on foot

Budapest's Best...
The best experiences

Survival Guide

Tips and tricks for a seamless, hassle-free city experience

Getting Around
Travel like a local

Essential Information
Including where to stay

Our selection of the city's best places to eat, drink and experience:

◉ Sights

✕ Eating

🍷 Drinking

⭐ Entertainment

🛍 Shopping

These symbols give you the vital information for each listing:

☎ Telephone Numbers	🚼 Family-Friendly
⊘ Opening Hours	🐾 Pet-Friendly
🅿 Parking	🚌 Bus
⊖ Nonsmoking	⛴ Ferry
@ Internet Access	Ⓜ Metro
🛜 Wi-Fi Access	Ⓢ Subway
🥗 Vegetarian Selection	🚃 Tram
📖 English Language Menu	🚆 Train

Find each listing quickly on maps for each neighbourhood:

Bar Hemingway

16 🚇 Map p233, B2

Legend has it that Hemi self, wielding a machine rate this timber-pan ered bar during showpiece is a en by Papa ar town. Dress s.com; Hôtel Rit ⊘6.30pm-2a

6 ◉ Plac V

Lonely Planet's Budapest

Lonely Planet Pocket Guides are designed to get you straight to the heart of the city.

Inside you'll find all the must-see sights, plus tips to make your visit to each one really memorable. We've split the city into easy-to-navigate neighbourhoods and provided clear maps so you'll find your way around with ease. Our expert authors have searched out the best of the city: walks, food, nightlife and shopping, to name a few. Because you want to explore, our 'Local Life' pages will take you to some of the most exciting areas to experience the real Budapest.

And of course you'll find all the practical tips you need for a smooth trip: itineraries for short visits, how to get around, and how much to tip the guy who serves you a drink at the end of a long day's exploration.

It's your guarantee of a really great experience.

Our Promise

You can trust our travel information because Lonely Planet authors visit the places we write about, each and every edition. We never accept freebies for positive coverage, so you can rely on us to tell it like it is.

QuickStart Guide 7

Explore Budapest 21

Worth a Trip:

The Best of Budapest 123

Budapest's Best Walks

Budapest's Best ...

Survival Guide 143

QuickStart Guide

Welcome to Budapest

Straddling the Danube with the Buda Hills as backdrop and boasting enough baroque, neoclassical and Art Nouveau architecture to satisfy anyone, Budapest is plentifully endowed with natural and human-made beauty. But the Queen of the Danube is not just a pretty face. At night she frocks up to become what is now the region's premier party town.

Széchenyi Baths (p119)
CHRISTIAN KOBER/GETTY IMAGES ©

Budapest Top Sights

Royal Palace (p24)

The focal point of Castle Hill in Buda and the city's most visited sight, the enormous Royal Palace contains two important museums, the national library and an abundance of notable statues and monuments.

GAVIN GOUGH/GETTY IMAGES ©

Basilica of St Stephen (p76)

Budapest's most important Christian house of worship is a gem of neoclassical architecture that took more than half a century to complete and contains the nation's most sacred object: the holy right hand of King St Stephen.

SPACES IMAGES /IMAGES/GETTY IMAGES ©

JEAN-PIERRE LESCOURRET/GETTY IMAGES ©

Gellért Baths (p40)

'Taking the waters' is very much a part of everyday life in Budapest and soaking in the Art Nouveau Gellért Baths, with temperatures of up to 38°C, has been likened to bathing in a cathedral.

Parliament (p74)

The centrepiece along
the Danube in Pest
and Hungary's largest
building, Parliament is
the seat of the National
Assembly and contains
the coronation regalia of
King Stephen.

Hungarian National Museum (p110)

Purpose built in 1847, the
Hungarian National Mu-
seum houses the nation's
most important collection
of historical relics, from
King Stephen's crimson
silk coronation mantle to
memorabilia from social-
ist times.

City Park (p118)

Pest's green lung, City
Park is an open space
measuring almost exactly
a square kilometre and
contains museums, gal-
leries, a zoo, a permanent
circus and one of the best
thermal baths in the city.

Memento Park (p48)

Containing garish statues and over-the-top memorials from the Communist period, Memento Park could be described as both a cemetery of socialist mistakes and a well-manicured trash heap of history.

Citadella & Liberty Monument (p38)

Built by the Habsburgs after the War of Independence, the Citadella atop Gellért Hill is a fortress that never saw battle. Nearby is the Liberty Monument, the lady with a palm frond proclaiming freedom throughout the city.

Aquincum (p58)

Today's Budapest was settled by the Romans at the end of the 1st century AD and Aquincum, the most complete civilian Roman town in Hungary, now contains an enclosed museum and an open-air archaeological park.

Great Synagogue (p94)

The largest Jewish temple in Europe, the Moorish-style Great Synagogue, with its iconic copper dome, is one of Budapest's most eye-catching and beloved buildings.

Budapest Local Life

Insider tips to help you find the real city

After taking in Budapest's fabulous array of sights, it's time to get behind what everyone sees in order to discover the Budapest local people know and love: the superb restaurants, the quirky shops and markets, and the bars and clubs that never say die.

Touring the Buda Hills (p60)

▶ Clear air
▶ Quirky transport

They may be short on sights, but the Buda Hills are a welcome respite from the hot, dusty city in summer. Perhaps their biggest draws are their unusual forms of transport: a 19th-century narrow-gauge cog railway, a train run by children and a chairlift that will get you back down to terra firma.

Bar-Hopping in Erzsébetváros (p96)

▶ Craft beers
▶ World-class wine

Don't just follow the herd when day becomes night in this super party town. We have the lowdown on where's the most fun with the least amount of hassle in the very heart of the nightlife area: Erzsébetváros.

Exploring Váci utca & Vörösmarty tér (p64)

▶ Top shops
▶ Beckoning cafes

Follow us on a walking tour of Budapest's premier shopping street that eschews the chain stores and brand-name shops in favour of more upscale local emporiums, notable buildings and smart cafes, including the iconic Gerbeaud, the capital's finest *cukrászda* (cake shop).

From Market to Market Around Southern Pest (p112)

▶ Local specialities
▶ Living history

In this tale of two markets – one a visitor's paradise, the other where auntie shops – we walk the backstreets, discovering everything from antiquarian bookshops and cool cafes to ghosts of the 1956 Uprising that still haunt the neighbourhood.

Erzsébetváros nightlife (p96)

Treat time at Gerbeaud (p65)

Other great places to experience the city like a local:

Szimpla Farmers' Market (p102)

BÁV (p83)

Császár-Komjádi Pools (II Árpád fejedelem útja 8; ⊙6am-7pm)

Pump Room (p44)

Károly Garden (p70)

Fortuna Önkiszolgáló (p32)

Bringóhintó (p89)

Ervin Szabó Central Library (www.fszek. hu; VIII Reviczky utca 1; ⊙10am-8pm Mon-Fri, to 4pm Sat)

LONELY PLANET/GETTY IMAGES ©

TIM E WHITE/GETTY IMAGES ©

Budapest Day Planner

Day One

Spend your first morning on Castle Hill, taking in the views from the **Royal Palace** (p24) and establishing the lay of the land. There are museums aplenty up here, but you probably only have time for one. We recommend either the **Hungarian National Gallery** (p25) for fine art or the rebranded **Castle Museum** (p27) for a painless introduction to the city's tortuous past. Have a quick bite at the upbeat self-service **Vár Bistro** (p32).

In the afternoon ride the **Sikló** (funicular; p25) down to Clark Ádám tér and, depending on the day of the week and your sex, make your way up Fő utca to the **Király Baths** (p30) for a relaxing soak or down to the **Gellért Baths** (p40). If you choose the second, the **Citadella** (p38) and **Liberty Monument** (p38) are just opposite. The superb **Csalogány 26** (p31) restaurant is around the corner from the Király Baths.

Depending on your mood, check to see what's on in the way of *táncház* (folk music and dance) at the **Marczibányi tér Cultural Centre** (p34) just north of Széll Kálmán tér or head for stylish **Oscar American Bar** (p61) south of the square for cocktails and canned music.

Day Two

On your second day day, cross the Danube and see Pest at its very finest by walking up leafy Andrássy út, which will take you past such unmissable sights as the **House of Terror** (p100) and **Heroes' Square** (p119), architectural gems like the **Hungarian State Opera House** (p100) and wonderful cafes including **Művész Kávéház** (p104) and **Alexandra Book Cafe** (p104). **Menza** (p103) has an excellent-value weekday set lunch.

As you approach City Park, decide whether you want an afternoon of culture or leisure (or both). Heroes' Sq is flanked by the **Museum of Fine Arts** (p119) and the **Palace of Art** (p120), both with excellent exhibitions, and City Park contains the **Budapest Zoo** (p119) and the wonderful **Széchenyi Baths** (p119). **Robinson** (p119) by the park's lake is a wonderful choice.

After that you might make your way down Andrássy út to Erzsébetváros and have drinks at always raucous **La Bodeguita del Medio** (p104). If it's a club night (usually salsa) stay on, or perhaps head for the basement club at **GMK** (p97) with its excellent sound system and a good reputation for quality DJs and live music.

Short on time?
We've arranged Budapest's must-sees into these day-by-day itineraries to make sure you see the very best of the city in the time you have available.

Day Three

In the morning concentrate on the two icons of Hungarian nationhood and the places that house them: the Crown of St Stephen in the **Parliament** (p74) and the saint-king's remains in the **Basilica of St Stephen** (p76). To get from one to the other cut through **Szabadság tér** (p80) and glimpse the city's last remaining Soviet memorial. **Kisharang** (p82) is an excellent choice for Hungarian soul food.

After lunch turn to the Jewish Quarter. Leave ample time to visit the **Great Synagogue** (p94) and the **Hungarian Jewish Museum** (p95) (and have a slice of something sweet at **Fröhlich Cukrászda** (p105) kosher cake shop). Alternatively, head over to the Belváros to explore Váci utca and Vörösmarty tér or down to the Nagycsarnok to visit the markets and sights of southern Budapest, making sure not to miss the **Hungarian National Museum** (p110). The **Spinoza Café** (p102) is a convivial place for an evening meal.

Spend the evening enjoying the wealth of *kertek* (garden clubs) within easy striking distance along Kazinczy utca, notably the granddaddy of them all, **Szimpla Kert** (p103).

Day Four

On your last day have a look at what the western side of the Danube used to be like by strolling through Óbuda and learning how Buda, Óbuda and Pest all came together. The **Vasarely Museum** (p54) and its hallucinogenic works never fail to please and the nearby **Hungarian Museum of Trade & Tourism** (p54) is a positive delight. Otherwise, **Aquincum** (p59) is just a short HÉV ride away. The fish soup at **Új Sípos Halászkert** (p56) goes down a treat.

In the afternoon head south for Margaret Bridge. Just up the hill to the west is **Gül Baba's Tomb** (p54), the only Muslim place of pilgrimage in northern Europe. Spend the rest of the afternoon at the **Veli Bej Baths** (p54). Alternatively, or if you've the luxury of another half-day up your sleeve, be sure to visit **Memento Park** (p49). **Földes Józsi Konyhája** (p56) is a fine and homey eatery just west of the baths.

Cross over Margaret Bridge to Margaret Island and **Holdudvar** (p90) bar-club. It's open till the wee hours, so there's no rush.

Need to Know

For more information, see Survival Guide (p144)

Currency
Forint (Ft); some hotels quote in euros (€)

Language
Hungarian (Magyar)

Visas
Generally not required for stays up to 90 days.

Money
ATMs are everywhere. Credit cards are accepted in most hotels, restaurants and shops.

Mobile Phones
Most North American phones don't work here. Consider buying a rechargeable SIM card if your phone is not locked.

Time
Central European Time (GMT/UTC plus one hour)

Plugs & Adaptors
Plugs have two round pins; electrical current is 230v/50hz.

Tipping
Hungarians are very tip-conscious and nearly everyone in Budapest will routinely hand gratuities to waiters, hairdressers and taxi drivers.

❶ Before You Go

Your Daily Budget

Budget less than 15,000Ft
► Dorm bed 2800–6000Ft
► Meal at self-service restaurant 1500Ft
► Three-day transport pass 4150Ft

Midrange 15,000–30,000Ft
► Single/double room from 7000/9500Ft
► Two-course meal with drink 3500–7500Ft
► Cocktail from 1300Ft

Top end more than 30,000Ft
► Dinner for two with wine from 12,500Ft
► Spa ticket adult/child 5300/3100Ft
► Cover at a popular club 2000–3500Ft

Useful Websites

► **Xpat Loop** (www.xpatloop.com) Popular English-language site, with local news, interviews, features and listings.

► **Caboodle** (www.caboodle.hu) Daily news, features, events and irreverent comment.

► **Budapest Info** (www.budapestinfo.hu) Official website of Budapest Tourism.

► **Lonely Planet** (www.lonelyplanet.com/budapest) Destination information, hotel bookings, traveller forum and more.

Advance Planning

Two months before Book your accommodation if travelling in the high season. Take a look at the 'what's on' and English-language media websites.

A month before Reserve seats for a big-ticket concert, musical or dance performance. Book top-end restaurants.

A week before Make sure your bookings are in order and you have all references.

② Arriving in Budapest

Most people arrive in Budapest by air, but you can also get here from dozens of European cities by bus and train and from Vienna by Danube hydrofoil.

✈ From Ferenc Liszt International Airport

For Pest (Deák tér), take the Airport Shuttle Minibusz, or Bus 200E to Kőbánya-Kispest metro station, then M3 metro to Deák tér.

For Buda (Széll Kálmán tér), take the Airport Shuttle Minibusz, or Bus 200E to Kőbánya-Kispest metro station, then M3 metro to Deák tér and M2 to Széll Kálmán tér.

🚆 From Keleti, Nyugati & Déli Train Stations

For Pest (Deák tér), take the M2 metro from Keleti pályaudvar and Déli pályaudvar, or the M3 metro from Nyugati pályaudvar.

For Buda (Széll Kálmán tér), take the M2 metro to Keleti pályaudvar and Déli pályaudvar, or the M3 metro from Nyugati pályaudvar then M3 metro to Széll Kálmán tér.

🚆 From Stadion & Népliget Bus Stations

Stadion and Népliget bus stations are on the M2 and M3 metro lines respectively, which go to Deák tér.

⚓ From International Ferry Pier

Vienna hydrofoils arrive at and depart from the International Ferry Pier, which is on tram 2 and near the Fővám tér station of the M4 metro.

③ Getting Around

Budapest has a safe, efficient and inexpensive public-transport system run by **BKK** (Budapesti Közlekedési Központ, Centre for Budapest Transport; ☎1-258 4636; www. bkk.hu). Five types of transport are in general use, but the most useful for travellers are the metro trains on four numbered and colour-coded city lines, blue buses and yellow trams. The basic fare for all forms of transport is 350Ft (3000Ft for a block of 10). There's a seven-day pass for 4950Ft.

Ⓜ Metro

Budapest has four underground metro lines. The M1, M2 and M3 converge at Pest's central Deák Ferenc tér (only), while the new M4 links to the M2 at Keleti pályaudvar and the M3 at Kálvin tér, both in Pest. The M2 reaches central Széll Kálmán tér in Buda, the M4 serves south Buda.

🚌 Bus & Tram

An extensive system of buses running on some 260 routes day and night serves greater Budapest. A bus with an 'E' after the number means it is express, making limited stops.

There are trams on 30 lines. They are often faster and generally more pleasant for sightseeing than buses.

🚕 Taxi

Taxis in Budapest are cheap by European standards, with uniform flag-fall at 450Ft and a per-kilometre charge of 280Ft.

Budapest Neighbourhoods

Óbuda (p50)

This is the oldest part of Buda and retains a lost-in-the-past village feel; here you'll find the remains of the Roman settlement of Aquincum and some legendary eateries.

Castle District (p22)

Castle Hill, nerve centre of Budapest's history and packed with important museums, is here, as is ground-level Víziváros, with some excellent restaurants.

◉ **Top Sights**

Royal Palace

Gellért Hill & Tabán (p36)

The Citadella and the Liberty Monument gaze down from atop Gellért Hill on the neighbourhood of the Tabán.

◉ **Top Sights**

Citadella & Liberty Monument

Gellért Baths

◉ Parliament

◉ Royal Palace

◉ Citadella & Liberty Monument

◉ Ge Bat

Margaret Island & Northern Pest (p84)

This unspoiled island in the Danube offers a green refuge, while northern Pest beckons with its shops and lovely cafes.

Parliament & Around (p72)

Takes in the areas around the Parliament building and the equally iconic Basilica of St Stephen, plus Nagymező utca, Budapest's Broadway.

⊙ Top Sights

Parliament

Basilica of St Stephen

City Park

Erzsébetváros & the Jewish Quarter (p92)

This neighbourhood offers the lion's share of Budapest's accommodation, restaurants serving every cuisine under the sun and the city's hottest nightspots.

⊙ Top Sights

Great Synagogue

Worth a Trip

⊙ Top Sights

Memento Park

Aquincum

Basilica of St Stephen

Great Synagogue

Hungarian National Museum

Southern Pest (p108)

Traditionally working class, this is an area to wander, poking your nose into courtyards and small, often traditional, shops.

⊙ Top Sights

Hungarian National Museum

lért ns

Belváros (p62)

The 'Inner Town' centres on touristy Váci utca, with its shops and bars, and Vörösmarty tér, home to the city's most celebrated *cukrászda* (cake shop).

Explore
Budapest

Worth a Trip

Sikló (funicular railway) climbs Castle Hill (p22)
RICHARD I'ANSON/GETTY IMAGES ©

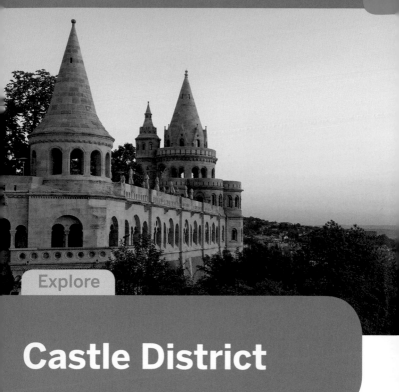

Explore

Castle District

Castle Hill (Várhegy) is a 1km-long limestone plateau towering 170m above the Danube. The premier sight in the capital, it contains Budapest's most important medieval monuments and museums in two distinct areas: the Royal Palace and the Old Town. Víziváros (Watertown) is the narrow area between the Danube and Castle Hill that spreads as far as Széll Kálmán tér, Buda's most important transport hub.

The Sights in a Day

You could spend an entire day or even longer on Castle Hill given the wealth of attractions here, but try to restrain yourself. Make your way up on the **Sikló** (p25) and choose either the **Hungarian National Gallery** (p25) or the **Castle Museum** (p27). Then walk over to **Fishermen's Bastion** (p30) to enjoy the views and peek inside **Matthias Church** (p30).

If you want something quick for lunch head for **Vár Bistro** (p32). Otherwise **Rivalda** (p32) is a lovely spot, especially in its courtyard in fine weather. After lunch, walk over to the **Hospital in the Rock** (p30) and join a tour of the underground passages. A visit to the Museum of Military History would tie up any loose ends, but some visitors may have had enough of war and opt for the more lyrical **Music History Museum** (p31).

In the late afternoon walk through Vienna Gate to **Oscar American Bar** (p33) for a libation. One of our favourite restaurants, **Csalogány 26** (p31), is within easy striking distance. And check out what's on at the **Marczibányi tér Cultural Centre** (p34) for later. If you're lucky a *táncház* (folk music and dance) session will be on the program.

Top Sights

Royal Palace (p24)

Best of Budapest

Eating

Csalogány 26 (p31)

Déryné (p32)

Drinking

Oscar American Bar (p33)

Ruszwurm Cukrászda (p33)

Museums & Galleries

Hungarian National Gallery (p25)

Castle Museum (p27)

Getting There

Funicular I Clark Ádám tér for Sikló to I Szent György tér.

Bus V Deák Ferenc tér in Pest for 16 to I Dísz tér.

Tram I Batthyány tér for 19 to I Szent Gellért tér and south Buda; 4 and 6 to Pest (Big Ring Rd).

Metro M2 Batthyány tér and Széll Kálmán tér.

Top Sights
Royal Palace

The enormous Royal Palace has been razed and rebuilt at least six times over the past seven centuries. Béla IV established a residence here in the mid-13th century and subsequent kings added to it. The palace was levelled in the battle to rout the Turks in 1686; the Habsburgs rebuilt it but spent very little time here. Today the palace contains two important museums, the national library and an abundance of statues and monuments.

◉ Map p28, E8

Királyi Palota

I Szent György tér

Royal Palace viewed from the Danube

Don't Miss

Ornamental Entrances

The complex has two entrances. The first is via the Habsburg Steps and through an ornamental gateway dating from 1903. The other way in is via Corvinus Gate, with its big black raven symbolising the Renaissance King Matthias Corvinus.

Hungarian National Gallery

The **Hungarian National Gallery** (Nemzeti Galéria; ☏1-201 9082; www.mng.hu; I Szent György tér 2, Buildings A-D; adult/concession 1400/700Ft, audioguide 800Ft; ⏱10am-6pm Tue-Sun; 🚌16, 16A, 116) spreads across four floors of four buildings, and traces Hungarian art from the 11th century to the present day. The largest collections include medieval and Renaissance stonework, Gothic wooden sculptures, late Gothic winged altars and late Renaissance and baroque art. The museum also has an important collection of 19th- and 20th-century art.

Gothic Works

The winged altarpieces in the so-called Great Throne Room (1st floor, Building D) date from the 15th and early 16th centuries and form one of the greatest collections of late Gothic painting in the world. *Visitation* (1506) by Master MS is both lyrical and intimate, but keep an eye open for the monumental Annunciation Altarpiece (1510–20).

Renaissance & Baroque Works

The finest 18th-century baroque painters in Hungary were actually Austrians, including Franz Anton Maulbertsch (1724–96; *Death of St Joseph*) and Stephan Dorfmeister (1725–97; *Christ on the Cross*). A Hungarian master is Jakob Bogdány (1660–1724; *Two Macaws, a Cockatoo and a Jay, with Fruit*). Their works are in the galleries adjoining the Great Throne Room.

ELLEN ROONEY/GETTY IMAGES ©

☑ Top Tips

▶ The most fun way to reach Castle Hill is to board the **Sikló** (I Szent György tér; one way/return adult 1100/1700Ft, child 650/1100Ft; 7.30am-10pm, closed 1st & 3rd Mon of month), a funicular railway built in 1870 that ascends from Clark Ádám tér at the western end of Chain Bridge to Szent György tér near the Royal Palace.

▶ Catch the low-key but ceremonial changing of the guard at Sándor Palace hourly between 9am and 6pm.

▶ If you want to leave Castle Hill after visiting the Castle Museum, exiting through the museum's back courtyard door will take you straight down to I Szarvas tér in the Tabán.

✗ Take a Break

If you just want something hot and/or sweet after your visit to the museum(s), head for Ruszwurm Cukrászda (p33).

HUNGARIAN NATIONAL GALLERY

Father & Uncle Piacsek
Drinking Red Wine ●
by Rippl-Rónai

*WWI Paintings
by Mednyánszky*

The Fair at Csikszereda
by Aba-Novák

**20th-Century
Painting & Sculpture
(to 1945)** ●

2nd Floor

**19th-Century
Painting &
Sculpture** ●

Ruins of the Greek Theatre at
Taormina & Pilgrimage to the
Cedars of Lebanon
by Csontváry

Temporary
Exhibitions

Great Throne Room ●
(*Gothic Altarpieces*)

*National
Romantic School
(Székely & Benczúr)*

● Works by
Szinyei Merse

● Works by
Munkácsy

●
**Renaissance
& Baroque
Paintings**

1st Floor

*Temporary
Exhibitions
Building C*

⬇

Building D

⬆

Building B

Building A
*Temporary
Exhibitions*

Ground Floor

Nineteenth-Century Works

Building C contains examples of the National Romantic School of paintings: *Women of Eger* by Bertalan Székely (1835–1910), *The Baptism of Vajk* by Gyula Benczúr (1844–1920). In Building B are works by Mihály Munkácsy (1844–1900; *Storm in the Puszta*), and by the impressionist Pál Szinyei Merse (1845–1920; *The Skylark*).

Twentieth-Century Works

Two greats working in the late 19th and early 20th centuries were Tivadar Kosztka Csontváry (1853–1919) and József Rippl-Rónai (1861–1927; *Father and Uncle Piacsek Drinking Red Wine*). The harrowing depictions of war by László Mednyánszky (1852–1919; *In Serbia*) and the colourful works of Vilmos Aba-Novák (1894–1941; *The Fair at Csikszereda*) are also in Building C, 2nd floor.

Castle Museum

The **Castle Museum** (Vármúzeum; ☎1-487 8800; www.btm.hu; I Szent György tér 2, Building E; adult/concession 1800/900Ft; ⏰10am-6pm Tue-Sun Feb-Oct, to 4pm Nov-Mar; 🚌16, 16A, 116, 🚃19, 41) explores Budapest's 2000-year history. Restored 15th-century palace rooms are in the basement. On the ground floor, exhibits showcase Budapest during the Middle Ages, with dozens of important Gothic statues, heads and fragments of courtiers, squires and saints. On the 1st floor '1000 Years of a Capital' takes a multimedia look at housing, ethnic diversity and religion over the centuries.

National Széchenyi Library

The **National Széchenyi Library** (Országos Széchenyi Könyvtár; ☎1-224 3700; www.oszk.hu; I Szent György tér 4-6, Building F; ⏰9am-8pm, stacks to 7pm Tue-Sat; 🚌16) contains codices and manuscripts, a large collection of foreign newspapers and a copy of everything published in Hungary or the Hungarian language. It was founded in 1802 by Count Ferenc Széchenyi, who endowed it with 15,000 books and 2000 manuscripts.

Matthias Fountain

Facing the Royal Palace's large courtyard to the northwest is the Romantic-style **Matthias Fountain** (Mátyás kút), portraying the young king Matthias Corvinus in hunting garb. To the right below him is Szép Ilona (Beautiful Helen). The middle one of the king's three dogs was blown up during the war; canine-loving Hungarians quickly had an exact copy made.

Statues & Monuments

Near the Habsburg Steps is a bronze statue of the **Turul**, a totemic bird important in Magyar folklore. In front of Building C is a statue of **Eugene of Savoy**, the Habsburg prince who wiped out the last Turkish army in Hungary at the Battle of Zenta in 1697. On the other side is a **Hortobágyi csikós**, a Hungarian cowboy in full regalia.

Understand
Tivadar Kosztka Csontváry

Many critics consider Tivadar Kosztka Csontváry – a symbolist artist whose tragic life is sometimes compared with that of his contemporary, Vincent van Gogh – to be Hungary's greatest painter. Csontváry produced his major works in just half a dozen years starting in 1903 when he was 50. His efforts met with praise at his first exhibition in 1907 in Paris, but critics panned his work at a showing in Budapest the following year. He died penniless just after WWI. View his works, including *Ruins of the Greek Theatre at Taormina* (1905) and *Pilgrimage to the Cedars of Lebanon* (1907), on the 1st floor of the Hungarian National Gallery's Building C.

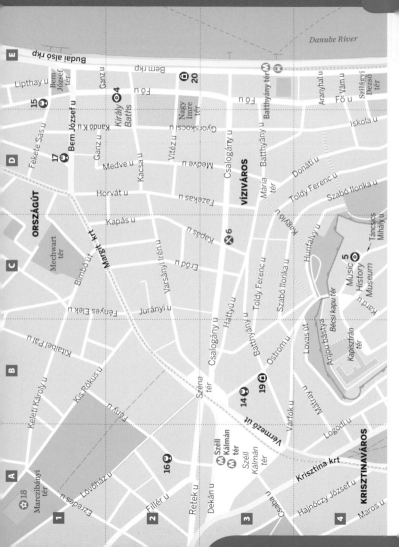

Danube River

Budai alsó rkp

Bem rkp

ORSZÁGÚT

VIZIVÁROS

KRISZTINAVÁROS

Lipthay u

Bem József tér

Ganz u

Fő u

Fő u

Aranyhal u

Vám u

Szilágyi Dezső tér

15

Fekete Sas u

Bem József u

Királý Baths

4

Kandó k u

Nagy Imre tér

Gyorskocsi u

Batthyány tér

Iskola u

17

Ganz u

Medve u

Kacsa u

Vitéz u

Csalogány u

Mária tér

Batthyány tér

Donáti u

20

Toldy Ferenc u

Szabó Ilonka u

Horvát u

Fazekas u

Medve u

Kapás u

Kapás u

6

Hattyú u

Kagyló u

Hunfalvy u

Táncsics Mihály u

Mechwart tér

Bimbó út

Margit krt

Erőd u

Varsányi Irén u

Toldy Ferenc u

Szabó Ilonka u

Music History Museum

5

Kard u

Anjou bástya

Fényes Elek u

Jurányi u

Csalogány u

Batthyány u

Ostrom u

Lovas út

Bécsi kapu tér

Kapisztrán tér

Kitaibel Pál u

Szena tér

14

19

Várfok u

Mátray u

Kelet Károly u

Kis Rókus u

Fény u

Vérmező út

Logodi u

Krisztina krt

Marczibányi tér

18

Ezredes u

Lövőház u

Fillér u

Retek u

Dékán u

Széll Kálmán tér

Széll Kálmán tér

16

Csaba u

Hajnóczy József u

Maros u

1

2

3

4

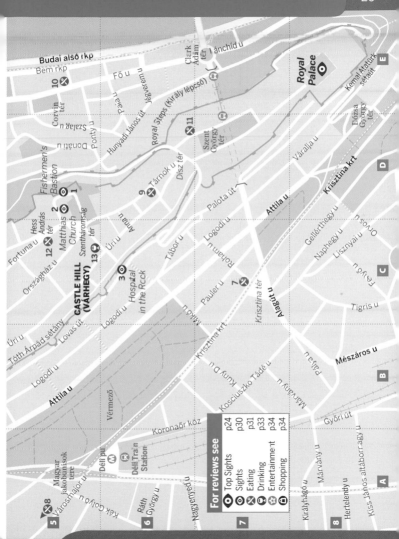

Budai alsó rkp
Bem rkp

10

Corvin tér

Fő u

Szalag u
Ponty u

Donáti u

Hunyadi János út

Royal Steps (Király lépcső)

Clark Ádám tér

Lánchíd u

Royal Palace

Kemal Atatürk sétaút

Szent György tér

11

Fishermen's Bastion

1

Tárnok u

Disz tér

Dózsa György tér

Hess András tér

2
Matthias Church

Szentháromság tér

Úri u

9

Anna u

Palota út

Váralja u

Krisztina krt

D

Fortuna u

12

Országház u

CASTLE HILL (VÁRHEGY)

13

Úri u

Logodi u

3

Hospital in the Rock

Tábor u

Roham u

Logodi u

Gellérthegy u

Attila u

Naphegy u

Lisznyai u

Olvos u

Fényő u

C

Úri u

Tóth Árpád sétány

Lovas út

Pauler u

7

Krisztina tér

Alagút u

Tigris u

Logodi u

Attila u

Vérmező

Mikó u

Krisztina krt

Kuny D. u

Mészáros u

Pálya u

B

Magyar Jakobinusok tere

8

Városmajor u

Koronaőr köz

Déli pu.

M

Déli Train Station

Kosciuszko Tádé u

Márvány u

Győri út

A

Kék Golyó u

Ráth György u

Nagyenyed u

For reviews see

⊙ Top Sights	p24	
⊙ Sights	p30	
⊗ Eating	p31	
⊕ Drinking	p33	
⊕ Entertainment	p34	
⊞ Shopping	p34	

7

Királyhágó u

Marvany u

Hertelendy u

Kiss János altborr.agy u

8

5

Sights

Fishermen's Bastion   MONUMENT

1 Map p28, D5

The bastion is a neo-Gothic masquerade that looks medieval and offers some of the best views in Budapest. Built as a viewing platform in 1905 by Frigyes Schulek, the architect behind Matthias Church, the bastion's name was taken from the medieval guild of fishermen responsible for defending this stretch of the castle wall. The seven gleaming white turrets represent the Magyar tribes that entered the Carpathian Basin in the late 9th century.

(Halászbástya; I Szentháromság tér; adult/concession 700/500Ft; ⏰9am-11pm mid-Mar–mid-Oct; 🚌16, 16A, 116)

☑ Top Tip
Lift Off

A real 'insider's' way to get to and from Castle Hill is from I Dózsa tér (bus 16 from Pest), where you'll find a **lift** (200Ft; ⏰6am-7pm Mon, to 8.30pm Tue-Sat, 9am-6.30pm Sun; 🚌16) that will whisk you up to the Lion Court and National Széchényi Library. You can also gain access via an escalator at the renovated Castle Bazaar (Várbazár) and royal gardens along the Danube bank.

Matthias Church   CHURCH

2 Map p28, D5

Parts of Matthias Church date back 500 years, notably the carvings above the southern entrance. But basically Matthias Church (so named because King Matthias Corvinus married Beatrix here in 1474) is a neo-Gothic confection designed by the architect Frigyes Schulek in 1896.

(Mátyás templom; 📞1-355 5657; www.matyas-templom.hu; I Szentháromság tér 2; adult/concession 1200/800Ft; ⏰9am-5pm Mon-Sat, 1-5pm Sun; 🚌16, 16A, 116)

Hospital in the Rock   MUSEUM

3 Map p28, C6

Part of the Castle Hill caves network, this subterranean hospital was used extensively during the WWII siege of Budapest and during the 1956 Uprising. It contains original medical equipment as well as some 200 wax figures and is visited on a guided one-hour tour, which includes a walk through a Cold War–era nuclear bunker and an eight-minute introductory video.

(Sziklakórház; 📞06 70 701 0101; www.sziklakorhaz.eu/en; I Lovas út 4/c; adult/6-25yr & senior 3600/1800Ft; ⏰10am-8pm; 🚌16, 16A, 116)

Király Baths   BATHHOUSE

4 Map p28, E2

The four pools here, with water temperatures of between 26°C and 40°C, are genuine Turkish baths erected in 1570 and have a wonderful skylit cen-

Matthias Fountain (p27)

tral dome (though the place is begging for a renovation). The Király is now open to both men and women every day of opening, so pack a swimsuit. (Király Gyógyfürdő; ☎1-202 3688; www.spasbudapest.com; II Fő utca 84; daily ticket incl cabin 2400Ft; ⊗9am-9pm; 🚌86, 🚊4, 6)

Music History Museum MUSEUM

5 Map p28, C4

Housed in an 18th-century palace with a lovely courtyard, this wonderful little museum traces the development of music in Hungary from the 18th century to the present day in a half-dozen exhibition rooms. There are rooms devoted to the work of Béla Bartók, Franz Liszt and Joseph Haydn,

with lots of instruments and original scores and manuscripts. (Zenetörténeti Múzeum; ☎1-214 6770; http://zti.hu/museum; I Táncsics Mihály utca 7; adult/child 600/300Ft; ⊗10am-4pm Tue-Sun; 🚌16, 16A, 116)

Eating

Csalogány 26 INTERNATIONAL €€€

6 Map p28, C3

Judged by Hungary's most respected food guide to be the best restaurant in town, this intimate place with the unimaginative name and spartan decor turns its creativity to its superb food. Try the suckling *mangalica* (a kind of pork) with Savoy cabbage (4500Ft)

Local Life
Self-Service Eatery

Locals working on Castle Hill avoid the generally overpriced spots frequented by tourists and eat at the self-service **Fortuna Önkiszolgáló** (I Fortuna utca 4; mains 700-1200Ft; 11.30am-2.30pm Mon-Fri). Cheap, cheerful and very convenient.

or the free-range pullet with polenta (3800Ft). A three-course set lunch is a budget-pleasing 2500Ft.
(📞1-201 7892; www.csalogany26.hu; I Csalogány utca 26; mains 3600-5000Ft; ⏰noon-3pm & 7-10pm Tue-Sat; 🚌11, 39)

Déryné   BISTRO €€

7 Map p28, C7

What was until not too long ago a traditional cafe near the entrance to the Alagút (the tunnel under Castle Hill) established the year WWI broke out has metamorphosed into a beautiful bistro with excellent breakfasts (890Ft to 2450Ft) and more substantial meals throughout the day. Great horseshoe-shaped bar and music, lovely terrace, open kitchen and a warm welcome.
(📞1-225 1407; www.bistroderyne.com; I Krisztina tér 3; mains 1780-4950Ft; ⏰7.30am-midnight Mon-Thu, to 1am Fri, 9am-1am Sat, to midnight Sun; 🚌16, 105, 178, 🚃18)

Fióka   HUNGARIAN €€

8 Map p28, A5

This newish bistro and wine bar gets the nod from the cognoscenti, who rave about the Hungarian duck and

pork dishes and the great selection of wines from not just Hungary but the whole Carpathian Basin. It's in a one-time office building near the foot of tiny Kissváb Hil.
(📞1-426 5555; www.fiokaetterem.hu; XII Városmajor utca 75; mains 2400-3600Ft; ⏰11am-midnight Wed-Sun)

Vár Bistro   HUNGARIAN €

9 Map p28, D6

This cheap and very cheerful self-service restaurant straddles the Royal Palace and the Old Town and is a good choice if you're looking for something fast and low priced. Salads are 650Ft to 990Ft and there's a two-course fixed 'tourist' menu for 1250Ft.
(📞06 30 237 0039; www.facebook.com/pages/Vár-Bistro/301382759927362; I Dísz tér 8; mains 1500-2400Ft; ⏰8am-9pm; 🚌16, 16A, 116)

Horgásztanya Vendéglő   FISH €€

10 Map p28, E5

A classic fish restaurant by the Danube where soup is served in bowls, pots or kettles, and your carp, catfish or trout might be prepared Baja-, Tisza- or more spicy Szeged-style.
(Fisherfarm Restaurant; 📞1-212 3780; www.horgasztanyavendeglo.hu; II Fő utca 20; mains 1550-2990Ft; ⏰noon-midnight; 🚌86)

Rivalda   INTERNATIONAL €€€

11 Map p28, D6

An international cafe-restaurant in a former convent next to the National Dance Theatre, Rivalda has a thespian

theme, a delightful garden courtyard and excellent service. The menu changes frequently, and the wine list is among the best. There's a four-course set menu for 13,200/8550Ft with/without wine.
(☎1-489 0235; www.rivalda.net; I Színház utca 5-9; mains 3100-5600Ft; ⏰11.30am-11.30pm; 🚌16, 16A, 116)

Vár: a Speiz   INTERNATIONAL €€€

12 🍴 Map p28, C5

Michelin may have taken its 'bib' away, but we still love this romantic bistro and its perennial warm welcome. Vár: a Speiz takes its food very seriously indeed and the five-course tasting menu (9800Ft) is memorable. It's just opposite the Hilton Budapest.
(Castle: The Pantry; ☎1-488 7416, www. varaspeiz.hu; I Hess András tér 6; mains 2800-4300Ft; ⏰noon-midnight; 🚌16, 16A, 116)

Drinking

Ruszwurm Cukrászda   CAFE

13 ☕ Map p28, C5

This diminutive cafe dating from 1827 is the perfect place for coffee and cakes (380Ft to 580Ft) in the Castle District, though it can get pretty crowded. Indeed, in high season it's almost always impossible to get a seat.
(☎1-375 5284; www.ruszwurm.hu; I Szentháromság utca 7; ⏰10am-7pm Mon-Fri, to 6pm Sat & Sun; 🚌6, 6A, 116)

Oscar American Bar   BAR

14 ☕ Map p28, B3

The decor is cinema inspired (film memorabilia on the wood-panelled walls, leather directors chairs...) and the beautiful crowd often act like they're on camera. Not to worry: the potent cocktails (1350Ft to 1750Ft) – from daiquiris and cosmopolitans to mojitos – go down a treat. There's music most nights.
(☎06 20 214 2525; www.oscarbar.hu; I Ostrom utca 14; ⏰5pm-2am Mon-Thu, to 4am Fri & Sat; Ⓜ M2 Széll Kálmán tér)

Bambi Presszó   CAFE

15 ☕ Map p28, E1

The words 'Bambi' and 'modern' do not make comfortable bedfellows; nothing about this place (named after a Communist-era local soft drink) has changed since the 1960s. And that's just the way the crowd here likes it. Friendly though set-it-down-with-a-crash service completes the picture.
(☎1-213 3171; www.facebook.com/bambieszpresszo; II Frankel Leó út 2-4; ⏰7am-10pm Mon-Fri, 9am-10pm Sat & Sun; 🚌86)

Auguszt Cukrászda   CAFE

16 ☕ Map p28, A2

Tucked away behind the Fény utca market and Mammut shopping mall complex, this is the original Auguszt (there are two newer branches in Pest) and it only sells its own shop-made cakes, pastries and biscuits. Seating is on the 1st floor.

Map p28, D1

Understand
Tánchaz

Attending a *tánchaz* (literally 'dance house' but really folk-music and dance workshops) is an excellent way to hear the music and and you can become part of the program as well instead of merely watching others perform. It's all good fun and they're easy to find in Budapest, where the dance-house revival began.

(☑1-316 3817; www.auguszt1870.hu; II Fény utca 8; cakes 260-640Ft; ☉10am-6pm Mon-Fri, from 10am Sat; Ⓜ M2 Széll Kálmán tér)

Score Club   GAY
17 Ⓟ Map p28, D1

We don't know whether the name is a threat or a promise, but Buda's only gay bar at the moment is a magnet for a slightly older crowd – not yet 'mature' but definitely no longer in short pants.
(☑06 20 341 4577; www.scoreclub.hu; II Tölgyfa utca 1-3; 1500-2000Ft; ☉10pm-6am Sat, 1 Fri per month; ☒4, 6)

Entertainment

Marczibányi tér
Cultural Centre   MUSIC
18 ⭐ Map p28, A1

This venue has Hungarian, Moldavian and Slovakian dance and music by

Guzsalyas every Thursday at 7pm and *tánchaz* (folk music and dance) every second Sunday at 1pm.
(Marczibányi téri Művelődési Központ; ☑1-212 2820; www.marczi.hu; II Marczibányi tér 5/a; performances 500-2000Ft; ☉from 8pm Wed; ☒4, 6)

Shopping

Bortársaság   WINE
19 🛍 Map p28, B3

Once known as the Budapest Wine Society, this place has 10 retail outlets across the capital, all of which feature an exceptional selection of Hungarian wines. No one, but no one, knows Hungarian wines like these guys do.
(☑1-212 0262; www.bortarsasag.hu; I Batthyány utca 59; ☉10am-7pm Mon-Fri, to 6pm Sat; Ⓜ M2 Széll Kálmán tér, ☒4, 6)

Herend Village Pottery   CERAMICS
20 🛍 Map p28, E2

An alternative to delicate Herend porcelain is the hard-wearing Herend pottery and dishes sold here, decorated with bold and colourful fruit and flower patterns. You can also enter this shop from II Fő utca 61.
(☑1-356 7899; www.herendimajolika.hu; II Bem rakpart 37; ☉9am-5pm Tue-Fri, to noon Sat; Ⓜ M2 Batthyány tér, ☒19, 41)

Understand

Hungarian Wine

Wine has been made in Hungary since at least the time of the Romans. It is very much a part of Hungarian culture, but only in recent years has it moved on from the local tipple you drank at Sunday lunch with the family or the overwrought and overpriced thimble of rarefied red sipped in a Budapest wine bar to the all-singin', all-dancin' obsession that it is today.

Wine Regions

Hungary is divided into seven wine-producing regions, but we're most interested in a half-dozen of their subdivisions. It's all a matter of taste, but the most distinctive (and big) Hungarian red wines come from Villány in Southern Transdanubia and Eger in the Northern Uplands. The reds from Szekszárd, also in Southern Transdanubia, are softer, more subtle. The best dry whites are produced around Lake Balaton's northern shore and in Somló, though the latest craze is for bone-dry, slightly tart Furmint from Tokaj, which also produces the world-renowned honey-sweet wine.

Buying & Choosing Wine

Wine is sold by the glass or bottle everywhere – usually at reasonable prices. Old-fashioned wine bars ladle out plonk by the *deci* (decilitre, or 0.1L), but if you're into more serious wine, you should visit one of Budapest's wine bars such as DiVino Borbár (p82), a wine restaurant like Klassz (p102) or speciality wine shops like the Bortársaság chain.

When choosing a Hungarian wine, look for the words *minőségi bor* (quality wine) or *különleges minőségű bor* (premium quality wine). On a wine label the first word indicates the region, the second the grape variety (eg Villányi Kékfrankos) or the type or brand of wine (eg Tokaji Aszú, Szekszárdi Bikavér). Other important words that you'll see include: *édes* (sweet), *fehér* (white), *félédes* (semisweet), *félszáraz* (semidry or medium), *pezsgő* (sparkling), *száraz* (dry) and *vörös* (red).

Wine & Food Pairing

Try a glass of Tokaji Aszú with savoury foods like *foie gras* or a strong cheese. A bone-dry Olaszrizling goes well with fish; pork dishes are nice with a new Furmint or any type of red, especially Kékfrankos. Hárslevelű goes well with poultry.

Explore

Gellért Hill & Tabán

Gellért Hill (Gellért-hegy) is a 235m-high rocky mound southeast of Castle Hill. Crowned with a fortress (of sorts) and the impressive Liberty Monument, it is Budapest's unofficial symbol. You can't beat the views of the Royal Palace or the Danube and its fine bridges from up here. The leafy area below the two hills is called the Tabán.

The Sights in a Day

☀️ Start the day with a climb up Gellért Hill to explore the **Citadella** (p38), admire the lovely lady proclaiming peace throughout the land and ogle the vistas. Walk down via the **St Gellért Monument** (p46) and stop in at the **Semmelweis Museum of Medical History** (p44) – always best visited on an empty stomach.

☀️ The **Aranyszarvas** (p44) is a relatively convenient place for lunch and an excellent choice in fine weather. Afterwards, depending on the day of the week and your sex, make your way to either the **Rudas Baths** (p44) or the **Gellért Baths** (p40) for a relaxing afternoon of soaking/and or swimming.

🌙 Wrap up your day with a cocktail or two at the **Szatyor Bár és Galéria** (p46). Later in the evening walk towards the Danube and board the **A38** (p46). You may never come ashore again.

👁 Top Sights

Citadella & Liberty Monument (p38)

Gellért Baths (p40)

❤️ Best of Budapest

Eating
Aranyszarvas (p44)

Drinking
A38 (p46)

Szatyor Bár és Galéria (p46)

Thermal Baths & Pools
Gellért Baths (p40)

Rudas Baths (p44)

Getting There

Ⓜ️ **Metro** M4 metro line, with stations at XI Gellért tér and XI Móricz Zsigmond körtér.

🚊 **Tram** Trams 47 and 49 from Pest. Tram 19 from I Batthyány tér in Buda.

🚌 **Bus** Bus 7 to XI Szent Gellért tér from V Ferenciek tere in Pest. Bus 27 to the top of Gellért Hill from XI Móricz Zsigmond körtér.

Top Sights
Citadella & Liberty Monument

The Citadella atop Gellért Hill is a fortress that never saw battle. Built by the Habsburgs after the 1848–49 War of Independence to defend the city from further insurrection, by the time it was ready two years later the political climate had changed and the Citadella had become obsolete. To the southeast stands the Liberty Monument, the lovely lady with a palm frond in her out-stretched arms proclaiming freedom throughout the city and the land.

⊙ Map p42, B3

www.citadella.hu

admission free

Interior of Cave Church

Don't Miss

Citadella

The Citadella is a U-shaped structure measuring 220m by 60m and built about a central courtyard. It was given to the city in the 1890s and parts of it were symbolically blown to pieces. Today the fortress contains some big guns peeking through the loopholes, but the interior has now been closed to the public and its future role remained a mystery at the time of publication.

Liberty Monument

Standing 14m high, the monument was erected in 1947 in tribute to the Soviet soldiers who died liberating Budapest in 1945. But the names of the fallen, once spelt out in Cyrillic letters on the plinth, and the statues of the soldiers themselves were removed in 1992 and sent to what is now called Memento Park (p49).

Cave Church

On the way up the hill on foot, have a peek at the Cave Church, built into a cavern in 1926 and the seat of the Pauline order here until 1951, when the priests were arrested and imprisoned by the Communists and the cave sealed off. It was reopened and reconsecrated in 1992. Behind it is a monastery with neo-Gothic turrets.

Liberty & Elizabeth Bridges

The spans below you are (to the south) Liberty Bridge and to the north Elizabeth Bridge. The former, which opened in time for the Millenary Exhibition in 1896, has a fin-de-siècle cantilevered span. Gleaming white Elizabeth Bridge, dating from 1964, enjoys a special place in the hearts of many Budapesters as it was the first newly designed bridge to reopen after WWII.

☑ Top Tips

▶ From the Citadella walk west for a few minutes along Citadella sétány to a lookout with one of the best vantage points in Budapest.

▶ To get to the Citadella on foot take the stairs leading up behind the St Gellért Monument or, from the Cave Church, follow XI Verejték utca (Perspiration St) through the park starting at the Cave Church.

▶ To avoid the steep climb, just hop on bus 27.

✖ Take a Break

Jubilee Park on the south side of Gellért Hill is an ideal spot for a picnic. Otherwise walk down the steps behind the St Gellért Monument and head north to Aranyszarvas (p44), especially if it's a fine day.

Top Sights
Gellért Baths

Soaking in the thermal waters of the Art Nouveau Gellért Baths, open to both men and women in mixed areas (thus a bathing suit is required at all times), has been compared to bathing in a cathedral. The eight thermal pools range in temperature from 26°C to 38°C, among the hottest in Budapest. The water – high in calcium, magnesium and hydrogen carbonate – is said to be good for joint pains, arthritis and blood circulation.

◉ Map p42, C4

Gellért gyógyfürdő

www.gellertbath.hu

XI Kelenhegyi út 4, Danubius Hotel Gellért

⊙ 6am-8pm

🚌 7, 86, Ⓜ M4 Szent Gellért tér, 🚋 18, 19, 47, 49

Patrons at Gellért Baths

Don't Miss

Art Nouveau Splendour

The Turks bathed here in the 16th century at what was called Sárosfürdő (Mud Bath) after the fine silt that was pushed up with the spring water. But the Gellért Baths as we know them today opened in 1918. That explains the splendour of the Art Nouveau mosaics and statues, Zsolnay ceramic fountains in the bathing pools and the glass-domed main indoor swimming pool.

In Hot Water

In most other baths nowadays you are given an electronic bracelet that directs you to and then opens your locker or cabin. The Gellért is still doing it the old way: you find a free locker or cabin yourself and – after you get changed in (or beside) it – you call the attendant, who will lock it for you and hand you a numbered tag.

Swimming Pools

The swimming pools at the Gellért are also mixed. The indoor ones, open year-round, are the most beautiful in Budapest; the outdoor wave pool (open May to September) has lovely landscaped gardens, where you can sunbathe or just while away a warm afternoon in summer.

WILL SANDERS/GETTY IMAGES ©

☑ **Top Tips**

▶ Along with a bathing suit you might bring with you a pair of flipflops and a towel as the sheets provided are not very absorbent.

▶ Everyone must use a bathing cap in the swimming pools; bring your own or wear the disposable one for 200Ft.

▶ Prices for the baths are: weekdays/weekends with locker 4900/5100Ft, or 5300/5500Ft for a cabin.

▶ Make sure you remember your locker number; the number on the tag is not the same as the one on the locker.

▶ It's customary to give the attendant a small tip.

✗ **Take a Break**

On XI Bartók Béla út, just around the corner from the baths, you'll find a number of eating options, including Marcello (p45), with great pizza and pasta dishes. For a coffee or a drink, Szatyor Bár és Galéria (p46) is a good choice.

43

For reviews see
- **◎** Top Sights   p38
- **◎** Sights   p42
- **✕** Eating   p44
- **◐** Drinking   p45
- **✿** Entertainment   p45

Budai alsó rkp

Petőfi Bridge
(Petőfi híd)

Műegyetem rkp

Egry József u

Bertalan Lajos u

Sztoczek József u

Irinyi József u

Egyetemisták parkja

Magyar tudósok körútja

Bogdányi u

FELSŐ-
LÁGYMÁNYOS

Budafoki út

Budafoki út

Orlay u

Zenta u

Lágymányosi u

Karinthy Frigyes út

Bercsényi u

Október 23 u

Baranyai u

Bocskai út

Fehérvári út

Mányoki út

Kelenhegyi út

Bartók Béla út

Himfy u

Móricz Zsigmond körtér

Mór cz Zsigmond kör-ér

Kőrösy József u

Eszék u

Október 23 u

Fadrusz u

Fadrusz u

Ménesi út

Fenekelten-tó

Balogh T u

SZENTIMRE-
VÁROS

Villányi út

Tas vezér u

Kosztolányi Dezső tér

Bocskai út

Ulászló u

Kanizsai u

Sárbogárdi út

Sights

Rudas Baths
BATHHOUSE

1 Map p42, C2

Built in 1566, these renovated baths are the most Turkish of all in Budapest, with an octagonal pool, domed cupola with coloured glass and massive columns. It's a real zoo on mixed weekend nights, when bathing costumes are compulsory. You can enter the lovely **swimming pool** (with locker weekday/weekend 2900/32000Ft, with thermal bath 3800/4100Ft; ⏰6am-8pm daily, 10pm-4am Fri & Sat) separately if you're more interested in swimming than soaking.

(Rudas Gyógyfürdő; ☎1-356 1322; www. spasbudapest.com; I Döbrentei tér 9; baths with cabin weekdays/weekends 3100/3400Ft, morning/night ticket 2400/4400Ft; ⏰men 6am-8pm Mon & Wed-Fri, women 6am-8pm Tue, mixed 10pm-4am Fri, 6am-8pm & 10pm-4am Sat & Sun; ☐7, 86, ☐18, 19)

Local Life
Drinking Cure

If you don't like getting wet or you don't have the time for a thermal bath, do what locals do and try a 'drinking cure' by visiting the **Pump Room** (I Erzsébet hid; ⏰11am-6pm Mon, Wed & Fri, 7am-2pm Tue & Thu), which is just below the western end of Elizabeth Bridge. A half-litre/litre of the hot, smelly water, which is meant to cure whatever ails you, is just 40/70Ft. Bring your own container.

Semmelweis Museum of Medical History
MUSEUM

2 Map p42, B1

This quirky (and sometimes grisly) museum traces the history of medicine from Graeco-Roman times through medical tools, instruments and photographs; yet another antique pharmacy also makes an appearance. Featured are the life and works of Ignác Semmelweis (1818–65), the 'saviour of mothers', who discovered the cause of puerperal (childbirth) fever. He was born here.

(Semmelweis Orvostörténeti Múzeum; ☎1-375 3533, 1-201 1577; www.semmelweis.museum.hu; I Apród utca 1-3; adult/child 700/350Ft; ⏰10.30am-6pm Tue-Sun mid-Mar–Oct, to 4pm Tue-Sun Nov–mid-Mar; ☐86, ☐19)

Eating

Aranyszarvas
HUNGARIAN €€€

3 Map p42, B1

Set in an 18th-century inn literally down the steps from the southern end of Castle Hill, the 'Golden Stag' serves up some very meaty and unusual dishes (try the saddle of boar with celeriac and sage or the duck breast with bok choy). The covered outside terrace is a delight in summer, and the views upward of the Royal Palace are sublime.

(☎1-375 6451; www.aranyszarvas.hu; I Szarvas tér 1; mains 3200-3800Ft; ⏰noon-11pm; ☐86)

DE AGOSTINI/GETTY IMAGES ©

Rudas Baths

Marcello

ITALIAN €

4 🍴 Map p42, C6

A perennial favourite with students from the nearby university since it opened more than two decades ago, this family-owned operation just down the road from XI Szent Gellért tér offers reliable Italian fare at affordable prices. The pizzas (1300Ft to 1800Ft) are good value, as is the salad bar, and the lasagne (1390Ft) is still legendary in these parts.

(📞1-466 6231; www.marcelloetterem.hu; XI Bartók Béla út 40; mains 1250-3980Ft; ⏲noon-10pm Mon-Sat; 🚊6)

Drinking

Tranzit Art Café

CAFE €

5 ☕ Map p42, A7

As chilled a place to drink and nosh as you'll find in south Buda, the Tranzit made its home in a small disused bus station, put art on the walls and filled the leafy courtyard with hammocks and comfy sofas. Breakfast and sandwiches are available, and two-course lunches (including a veggie one) can be had for 1200Ft during the week.

(📞1-209 3070; www.tranzitcafe.com; XI Bukarest utca & Ulászló utca; ⏲9am-11pm Mon-Fri, 10am-10pm Sat; 🚊7, 🚋19, 49)

Understand
St Gellért

Looking down on Elizabeth Bridge from Gellért Hill is a large and quite theatrical **monument to St Gellért** (🚌86, 🚌18, 19), an Italian missionary invited to Hungary by King Stephen to convert the natives. The monument marks the spot where, according to legend, pagan Magyars, resisting the new faith, hurled the bishop to his death in a spiked barrel in 1046.

A38
BAR, CLUB

6 🚋 Map p42, E6

Moored on the Buda side just south of Petőfi Bridge, the 'A38 Ship' is a decommissioned Ukrainian stone hauler from 1968 that has been recycled as a major live-music venue. It's so cool that Lonely Planet readers online voted it the best bar in the world. Surprised us too. The ship's hold rocks throughout the year.
(☎1-464 3940; www.a38.hu; XI Pázmány Péter sétány 3-11; ⏰11am-4pm, terraces 4pm-4am Tue-Sat; 🚌906, 🚌4, 6)

Szatyor Bár és Galéria
BAR

7 🚋 Map p42, C5

Sharing the same building as the **Hadik Kávéház cafe** (☎1-279 0291; www. hadikkavehaz.com; XIII Bartók Béla út 36; ⏰9am-11pm; Ⓜ M4 Móricz Zsigmond körtér, 🚌18, 19, 47, 49) and separated by just a door, the Szatyor is the funkier of the twins, with cocktails, street art on the walls and a Lada driven by the poet Endre Ady. Cool or what?
(Carrier Bag Bar & Gallery; ☎1-279 0290; www.szatyorbar.com; XIII Bartók Béla út 36-38; ⏰noon-1am Mon-Fri, 2pm-1am Sat & Sun; Ⓜ M4 Móricz Zsigmond körtér, 🚌18, 19, 47, 49)

Entertainment

Municipal Cultural House
MUSIC

8 ⭐ Map p42, B8

There's folk music and dance at what is also called the Folklore Theatre (Folklór Színház) on alternate Mondays, Fridays and Saturdays (see the website) at 7pm. A children's dance house hosted by the incomparable folk group Muzsikás runs every Tuesday from 5pm to 7pm.
(Fővárosi Művelődési Háza (FMH); ☎1-203 3868; www.fmhnet.hu; XI Fehérvári út 47; ⏰box office 3-7pm Mon, 3-6pm Tue, 1-6pm Wed & Thu, 4-6pm Fri; 🚌18 or 41)

Understand

Art Nouveau Architecture

Art Nouveau architecture and its Viennese variant, Secessionism, abound in Budapest. Examples can be spotted throughout the city, their sinuous curves, flowing, asymmetrical forms, colourful tiles and other decorative elements beckoning like beacons in a sea of refined and elegant baroque and mannered neoclassical buildings.

Art Nouveau was an art form and architectural style that flourished in Europe and the USA from 1890 to around 1910. It began in Britain as the Arts and Crafts Movement founded by William Morris (1834–96), which stressed the importance of manual processes and attempted to create a new organic style in direct opposition to the imitative banalities spawned by the Industrial Revolution.

The style soon spread to Europe, where it took on distinctly local and/or national characteristics. In Vienna a group of artists called the Secessionists lent its name to the more geometric local style of Art Nouveau architecture: Sezessionstil (Hungarian: Szecesszió). In Budapest, the use of traditional facades with allegorical and historical figures and scenes, folk motifs and Zsolnay ceramics and other local materials led to an eclectic, uniquely Hungarian style.

By the start of the 20th century, however, Art Nouveau and its variants were considered limited, passé, even tacky. Fortunately, the economic and political torpor of the interwar period and the 40-year 'big sleep' after WWII left many Art Nouveau/Secessionist buildings beaten but still standing – a lot more, in fact, than remain in such important Art Nouveau centres as Paris, Vienna and Brussels.

The master of the Hungarian version was Ödön Lechner (1845–1914): his most ambitious work in Budapest is the Museum of Applied Arts (p115), but his chef d'oeuvre is the Royal Postal Savings Bank (p80). Art Nouveau structures by others worth noting include the sumptuous interiors of the Gellért Baths (p40) and the Liszt Academy (p106), the Párisi udvar arcade (p64) and the Philanthia shop (p65).

Top Sights
Memento Park

Getting There

Ⓜ M4 to Kelenföld pályaudvar, then bus 101 or 150 to Buda-tétény vasútállomás (Campona).

🚌 The direct park bus departs from Le Meridien Budapest hotel on V Deák Ferenc tér.

Home to more than 40 statues, busts and plaques of Lenin, Marx, Engels, home-grown heroes such as Béla Kun, superhuman workers and others whose likenesses have ended up in dust bins or on trash heaps in other countries of the region, this socialist Disneyland, 10km southwest of the city centre, is truly a mind-blowing place to visit. It's a worthwhile and easy half-day trip out of the centre and can be easily reached by public transport from south Buda or on the park's own coach from Belváros in Pest.

Communist-era statue, Memento Park

Don't Miss

The Monuments
Ogle the socialist realism and try to imagine that at least four of these monstrous relics were erected as recently as the late 1980s; a few of them, including the Béla Kun memorial of our 'hero' in a crowd by fence-sitting sculptor Imre Varga, were still in place when your humble author moved to Budapest in 1992.

Old Barracks Exhibition
An exhibition centre in an old barracks has displays on the events of 1956 and the changes since 1989, and a documentary film with rare footage of secret agents collecting information on 'subversives'. The 'Communist Hot Line' allows you to listen in on the likes of Lenin, Stalin and even Che Guevara.

Stalin's Boots
Excellent selfie ops include the reproduced remains of Stalin's boots (all that was left after a crowd pulled the enormous statue down from its plinth on XIV Dózsa György út during the 1956 Uprising) and an original two-stroke Trabant, the 'people's car' produced in East Germany.

Shop
Not that we normally recommend museum gift shops, but this one is a treasure trove of kitsch communist memorabilia: pins, CDs of revolutionary songs, books and posters.

☏1 424 7500

www.mementopark.hu

XXII Balatoni út 16

adult/student
1500/1000Ft

⊙10am–dusk

☑ Top Tips

▶ Book tickets online and get a 25% discount.

▶ If you go via public transport the website offers a Memento Park Bonus Tour of sights to follow along the way, including vintage *sörözők* (pubs), a military cemetery with the graves of American soldiers killed in Hungary during WWII and a plethora of Soviet-style apartment blocks.

✕ Take a Break

Apart from a snack bar, catering facilities are rather thin on the ground at the park. We recommend taking a picnic or having lunch or a snack before you set out at one of the places in south Buda near the M4 such as the Tranzit Art Café (p45).

Explore

Óbuda

Ó means 'ancient' in Hungarian, so no prizes for guessing that Óbuda is the oldest part of Buda. At first glance the district doesn't look too promising. But behind all the prefabricated housing blocks and the massive flyover are some of the most important Roman ruins in Hungary, plus museums and small, quiet neighbourhoods that recall a distant past.

The Sights in a Day

☀ Start the day with a wake-up splash at the **Veli Bej Baths** (p54) and then fritter the morning away jumping in and out of the various pools and just relaxing. If you feel up to it, climb the hill a short distance to the west to view **Gül Baba's Tomb** (p54). It's a unique sight in this part of Europe.

☀ If you are ravenous after all that swimming and climbing, enjoy some tapas at **Pata Negra** (p56). Otherwise carry on by bus 86 to III Szentlélek tér for some fish soup at **Új Sípos Halászkert** (p56). Then take a closer look at fin-de-siècle Óbuda. Both the **Vasarely Museum** (p54) and the **Hungarian Museum of Trade & Tourism** (p54) deserve your attention

☾ Check to see what's playing at the **Óbuda Society** (p56) and plan your evening accordingly. **Kéhli Vendéglő** (p55) is just next door – convenient if you want to eat before or just after the performance. Otherwise make your way northeast to **Kisbuda Gyöngye** (p55), which remains the best restaurant in this neighbourhood.

 Best of Budapest

Food
Kisbuda Gyöngye (p55)

Museums & Galleries
Vasarely Museum (p54)

Hungarian Museum of Trade & Tourism (p54)

Getting There

🚌 **Bus** Bus 86 links XI Szent Gellért tér and other points in south Buda with III Flórián tér in Óbuda.

🚋 **Tram** Trams 1 and 1A run along the Outer Ring Rd (eg XIII Róbert Károl körút) from City Park in Pest to Árpád Bridge east of III Flórián tér in Óbuda. Tram 17 links II Margit körut with III Bécsi út.

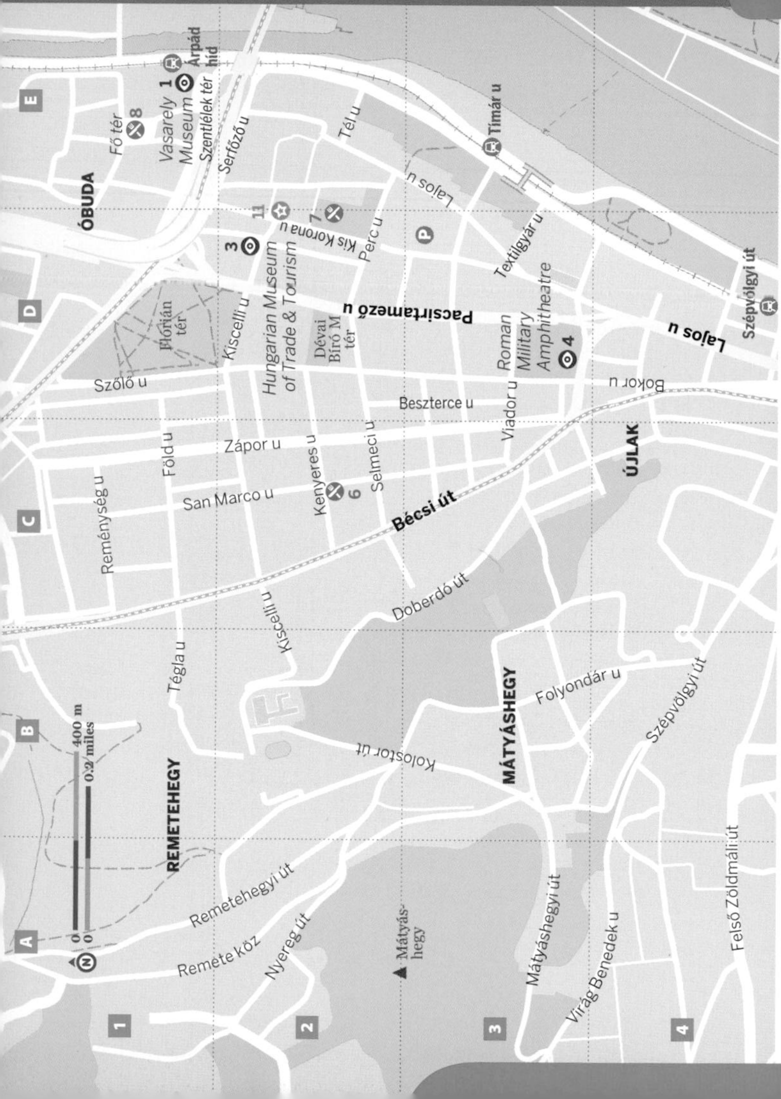

E

ÓBUDA

Fő tér

Vasarely **1**
Museum
Szentlélek tér
Árpád híd

Serfőző u

Tél u

Timár u

Lajos u

8

11

7

3

Kis Korona u

Perc u

Hungarian Museum
of Trade & Tourism

Kiscelli u

Flórián tér

Dévai
Bíró M
tér

D

Szőlő u

Pacsirtamező u

Textilgyár u

Roman
Military
Amphitheatre

4

Lajos u

Bokor u

Szépvölgyi út

Beszterce u

Viador u

Föld u

Zápor u

Kenyeres u

Selmeci u

San Marco u

6

Reménység u

Bécsi út

ÚJLAK

C

Kiscelli u

Doberdó út

Tégla u

Kolostor út

MÁTYÁSHEGY

Folyondár u

Szépvölgyi út

B

400 m

0.2 miles

REMETEHEGY

Remetehegyi út

Nyereg út

▲ Mátyás-
hegy

Mátyáshegyi út

Virág Benedek u

Felső Zöldmáli út

Remete köz

A

1

2

3

4

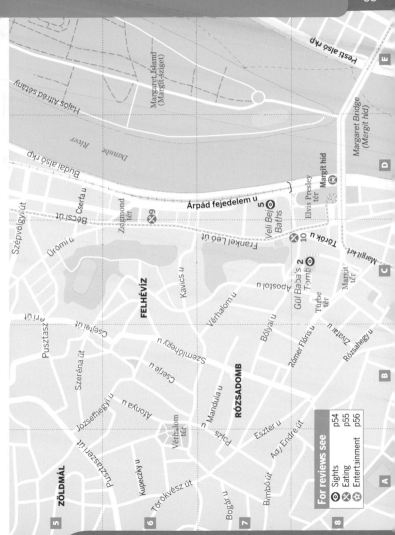

Margaret Island (Margit-sziget)

Pesti alsó rkp

Hajós Alfréd sétány

Margaret Bridge (Margit híd)

Danube River

Budai alsó rkp

Cserfa u

Bécsi út

Szépvölgyi út

Zsigmond tér

Árpád fejedelem u

Üröm u

Margit híd

Elvis Presley tér

Veli Bej Baths 5

Frankel Leó út

Török u 10

Margit krt

Kavics u

FELHÉVIZ

Gül Baba's 2 Tomb

Apostol u

Várhalom u

Thube tér

Margit tér

Pusztasz...

Csejtei út

Szemlőhegy u

Cserje u

Bólyai u

Rómer Flóris u

Zivatar u

Rózsahegy u

Szeréna út

Áfonya u

Mandula u

RÓZSADOMB

Józsehegyi...

Vérhalom tér

Páljs u

Eszter u

Ady Endre út

Pusztaszeri út

ZÖLDMÁL

Kupeczky u

Törökvész út

Bimbó út

Bogár u

Sights

Vasarely Museum
GALLERY

1 ⊙ Map p52, E1

Installed in the imposing Zichy Mansion (Zichy kastély) built in 1757, this museum contains the works of Victor Vasarely (or Vásárhelyi Győző as he was known before he emigrated to Paris in 1930), the late 'father of op art'. The works, are excellent and fun to watch as they 'swell' and 'move' around the canvas.
(⊘1-388 7551; www.vasarely.hu; III Szentlélek tér 6; adult/child 800/400Ft; ⊙10am-5.30pm Tue-Sun; ⊒86, ⊠HÉV Árpád híd)

Gül Baba's Tomb
ISLAMIC

2 ⊙ Map p52, C8

This reconstructed tomb contains the mortal remains of Gül Baba, an Ottoman dervish who took part in the capture of Buda in 1541 and is known in Hungary as the 'Father of Roses'. The tomb and mosque are a pilgrimage place for Muslims, and you must remove your shoes before entering. From Török utca, which runs parallel to Frankel Leó út, walk up steep Gül Baba utca to the set of steps just past No 16.
(Gül Baba türbéje; ⊘1-237 4400; www.museum.hu/budapest/gulbabaturbe; II Türbe tér 1; admission free; ⊙10am-6pm; ⊒4, 6 or 17)

Hungarian Museum of Trade & Tourism
MUSEUM

3 ⊙ Map p52, D2

One of our favourite small museums in Budapest, this unusual one looks at the catering and hospitality trade, with restaurant items, tableware, advertising posters, packaging and original shop signs. Go upstairs for an intimate look at the lives of various tradespeople – from bakers and publicans to launderers. The cafe is lit by antique lamps.
(Magyar Kereskedelmi és Vendéglató-ipari Múzeum; ⊘1-375 6249; www.mkvm.hu; III Korona tér 1; adult/child 800/400Ft; ⊙10am-6pm Tue-Sun; ⊒86, ⊠HÉV to Tímár utca)

Roman Military Amphitheatre
ARCHAEOLOGICAL SITE

4 ⊙ Map p52, D3

Built in the 2nd century for the Roman garrisons, this amphitheatre, about 800m south of Flórián tér, could accommodate 6000 spectators. The rest of the military camp extended north to Flórián tér. Take bus 86 to Flórián tér and get off at III Nagyszombat utca.
(Római Katonai Amfiteátrum; III Pacsirtamező utca; ⊒86, ⊠HÉV to Tímár utca)

Veli Bej Baths
BATHHOUSE

5 ⊙ Map p52, D7

One of the oldest (1575) and most beautiful Ottoman-era baths in Budapest has now come back to life after a complete renovation in 2011. The central cupola is surrounded by four smaller domed buildings, creating a total of five thermal pools. The water, pumped in at 38°C through original clay pipes, is high in sodium, potassium and calcium and good for joint ailments, chronic arthritis and calcium deficiency.

Gül Baba's Tomb

(Veli Bej Fürdője; ☑06 30 996 7255, 1-438 8641; www.irgalmas.hu/veli-bej-furdo; II Árpád fejedelem útja 7 & Frankel Leó út 54; 3-7pm 2800Ft, 6am-noon 2240Ft, after 7pm 2000Ft; ⊙6am-noon & 3-9pm; ☐86, ☐4, 6 ,17)

Eating

Kisbuda Gyöngye HUNGARIAN €€€

 6 ☒ Map p52, C2

Operating since the 1970s, this traditional Hungarian restaurant has an antique-cluttered dining room and attentive service, and has a *fin-de-siècle* atmosphere. Try the goose-liver speciality plate with a glass of Tokaj (3980Ft), or roast duck with apples (2980Ft), which is still out of this world.

(☑1-368 6402; www.remiz.hu; III Kenyeres utca 34; mains 2780-4980Ft; ⊙noon-3pm & 7-10pm Tue-Sat; ☐160, 260, ☐17)

Kéhli Vendéglő HUNGARIAN €€

7 ☒ Map p52, D2

Self-consciously rustic, Kéhli has some of the best traditional Hungarian food in town. One of Hungary's best-loved writers, the novelist Gyula Krúdy (1878–1933), who lived in nearby Dugovics Titusz tér, moonlighted as a restaurant critic and enjoyed Kéhli's *forró velőscsont pirítóssal* (bone marrow on toast; 990Ft) so much that he included it in one of his novels.

(☑1-368 0613; www.kehli.hu; III Mókus utca 22; mains 1990-4990Ft; ⊙noon-midnight; ☐86)

> ### Understand
> ## Budan: Buda Alaturka
>
> The Turks did little building in what they called Budan, apart from several bath-houses still extant (Király, Rudas), dervish monasteries, and tombs, city walls and bastions; for the most part, they used existing civic buildings for administration and converted churches into mosques. Matthias Church on Castle Hill, for example, was hastily turned into the Büyük Cami (Great Mosque), and the heart of the Royal Palace became a gunpowder store and magazine.

Új Sípos Halászkert   HUNGARIAN €€

 8   Map p52, E1

This old-style eatery faces (and, in the warmer weather, has outside seating in) Óbuda's most beautiful and historical square. Try the signature *halászlé* (fish soup; 1190Ft to 2490Ft); as the restaurant's motto says: *Halászlében verhetetlen* (You can't beat fish soup). Good vegetarian options, too.
(📞1-388 8745; www.ujsipos.hu; III Fő tér 6; mains 1590-3690Ft; ⏰noon-11pm Mon-Fri, to midnight Sat; 🖊; 🚊86)

Pata Negra   SPANISH €€

 9   Map p52, D6

The 'Black Foot' is a lovely Spanish tapas bar and restaurant and a much-needed addition to this district in Buda. The decor is fine, and the floor tiles and ceiling fans help create a mood *à la valenciana*. Good cheese and an excellent wine selection.
(📞1-438 3227; www.patanegra.hu; III Frankel Leó út 51; tapas 380-1150Ft, plates 840-2200Ft; ⏰11am-midnight; 🚊17)

Földes Józsi Konyhája   HUNGARIAN €€

10   Map p52, C8

This rustic little place just opposite the Lukács Baths was established by former hotel chef Joe Earthy – hey, that's what his name means! – a few years back and still serves excellent Hungarian home-style dishes including a good range of *főzelék* (vegetables in a roux; 690Ft to 750Ft).
(www.foldesjozsikonyhaja.hu; Frankel Leó út 30-34; mains 1900-2400Ft; ⏰11.30-3.30pm Mon, to 10pm Tue-Sat, noon-3.30pm Sun; 🚊4, 6, 17)

Entertainment

Óbuda Society   CONCERT VENUE

11   Map p52, D2

This very intimate venue in Óbuda takes its music very seriously and hosts recitals and some chamber orchestras. Highly recommended.
(Óbudai Társaskör; 📞1-250 0288; www.obudaitarsaskor.hu; III Kis Korona utca 7; tickets 800-3500Ft; 🚊86, 🚆HÉV to Tímár utca)

Understand

Music in Hungary

Hungary's contribution to music – especially the classical variety, called *komolyzene* (serious music) in Hungarian – belies the size of the country and its population. Of particular note and interest is Hungarian folk music, which has enjoyed something of a renaissance over the past few decades.

Classical Music

One person stands head and shoulders above the rest in this regard: Franz (or, in Hungarian, Ferenc) Liszt (1811–86). Liszt established the Academy of Music in Budapest and liked to describe himself as 'part Gypsy'. Some of his works, notably his 20 Hungarian Rhapsodies, do in fact echo the traditional music of the Roma.

Ferenc Erkel (1810–93) is the father of Hungarian opera, and two of his works – *Bánk Bán*, based on József Katona's play of that name, and *László Hunyadi* – are standards at the Hungarian State Opera House.

Béla Bartók (1881–1945) and Zoltán Kodály (1882–1967) made the first systematic study of Hungarian folk music, travelling together and recording throughout the Magyar linguistic region in 1906. Both incorporated their findings into their music – Bartók in *Bluebeard's Castle*, for example, and Kodály in the Peacock Variations.

Folk Music

It's important to distinguish between 'Gypsy' music and Hungarian folk music. Gypsy music as it is heard in Hungarian restaurants everywhere is based on tunes called *verbunkos* played during the Rákóczi independence wars. Fiddles, a bass and a cymbalom (a stringed instrument played with sticks) are de rigueur. Listen to anything by Sándor Lakatos and his band.

Hungarian folk musicians play violins, zithers, hurdy-gurdies, bagpipes and lutes on a five-tone diatonic scale. Watch out for Muzsikás; Marta Sebestyén; Ghymes, a Hungarian folk band from Slovakia; and the Hungarian group Vujicsics, which mixes elements of South Slav music.

Roma – as opposed to Gypsy – music is different altogether, and traditionally sung a cappella. Some modern Roma music groups – Kalyi Jag (Black Fire) from northeastern Hungary, Romano Drom (Gypsy Road) and Romani Rota (Gypsy Wheels) – have added guitars, percussion and even electronics to create a whole new sound.

Top Sights
Aquincum

Getting There

🚌 Nos 34 and 106 go to Aquincum from III Szentlélek tér in Óbuda.

🚆 The HÉV suburban train line links stations in Buda (Batthyány tér) and Óbuda (Szentlélek tér) with Aquincum.

Aquincum, dating from the end of the 1st century AD and the most complete Roman civilian town in Hungary, had paved streets and sumptuous single-storey houses, complete with courtyards, fountains and mosaic floors, as well as sophisticated drainage and heating systems. Not all of that is immediately apparent as you walk among the ruins in the open-air archaeological park, but the newly built museum will put it all in perspective.

Aquincum Roman ruins

Don't Miss

Aquincum Museum

The Aquincum Museum, on the southwestern edge of the Roman civilian settlement, contains a vast collection of coins and wall paintings and some tremendous virtual games for kids such as battling with a gladiator in the basement. Look out for the replica of a 3rd-century portable organ called a hydra, the mock-up of a Roman bath and a road map of the Roman Empire (*Tabula Peutingeriana*).

Painter's House & Mithraeum

Just opposite the exhibition hall is the wonderful Painter's House, a re-created Roman dwelling from the 3rd century AD. Behind it is the Mithraeum, a temple dedicated to the god Mithra, the chief deity of a religion that once rivalled Christianity.

Main Thoroughfare

Just north of the museum, the arrow-straight main thoroughfare leads you past ruins of the large public baths, the *macellum* (market) and the *basilica* (court house). Most of the large stone sculptures and sarcophagi are in the old museum building to the east.

Roman Civilian Amphitheatre

Across III Szentendrei út to the northwest and close to the HÉV stop is the Roman Civilian Amphitheatre, about half the size of the amphitheatre reserved for the garrisons in Óbuda and seating 3000. Lions were kept in the small cubicles, while slain gladiators were carried through the 'Gate of Death' to the west.

Aquincumi Múzeum

www.aquincum.hu

III Szentendre út 133-135

adult/student & senior 1600/800Ft, archaeological park only 1000/500Ft

⊙museum 10am-6pm Tue-Sun Apr-Oct, to 4pm Nov-Mar, park 9am-6pm Tue-Sun Apr-Oct

☑ Top Tips

▶ If travelling to Aquincum on the HÉV suburban train, view the Roman Civilian Amphitheatre first before crossing busy III Szentendre út.

▶ Be aware that tickets are *always* checked by a conductor on the HÉV.

▶ If you bought a ticket to the Castle Museum it is valid for entry to the Aquincum Museum for 30 days.

✗ Take a Break

A branch of the immensely popular Nagyi Palacsintázója pancake chain is at the entrance to the Aquincum Museum.

Local Life
Touring the Buda Hills

Getting There

Ⓜ Széll Kálmán tér metro station (M2).

🚌 59 or 61 to the Cog Railway lower terminus.

🚌 291 from the Chairlift terminus to II Szilágyi Erzsébet fasor.

Visitors to Budapest head for the hills – the city's 'green lungs' – for a variety of reasons. There's great hiking, a couple of trip-worthy sights and the summer homes of well-heeled Budapest families to ogle. But locals come just to ride the unusual forms of transport on offer. It really can be said that getting to/from the Buda Hills is half the fun.

1 Cog Railway Up

From Széll Kálmán tér metro station walk westward along Szilágyi Erzsébet fasor for 10 minutes (or take tram 59 or 61 for two stops) to the lower terminus of the **Cog Railway** (Fogaskerekű vasút; www.bkv.hu; Szilágyi Erzsébet fasor 14-16; admission 1 BKV ticket or 350Ft; ☾5am-11pm) just opposite the circular Hotel Budapest at No 47. Built in 1874, the railway climbs for 3.7km in 15 minutes three or four times an hour to Széchenyi-hegy (427m).

2 Picnic on Széchenyi-hegy

Here you can stop for a picnic (**Fény utca market** (II Fény utca; ☾6am-6pm Mon-Fri, to 2pm Sat) next to the Mammut shopping mall in II Széll Kálmán tér has supplies) in the attractive park south of the old-time station. Inside the station there's a tiny Cog Railway Museum (admission 50Ft) with great old memorabilia and photos.

3 Children's Railway

Just south on Hegyhát út opposite Rege út is the narrow-gauge **Children's Railway** (Gyermekvasút; ☎1-397 5394; www.gyermekvasut.hu; adult/child 1 section 600/300Ft, entire line 700/350Ft; ☾closed Mon Sep-Apr). Built in 1951 by Pioneers (socialist Scouts) and now staffed entirely by schoolchildren aged 10 to 14 (the engineer excluded), the little train chugs along for 11km, terminating at Hűvösvölgy 45 minutes later.

4 View from Elizabeth Lookout

Trails fan out from any of the eight stops along the railway line or you can return to Széll Kálmán tér on tram 61 from Hűvösvölgy. Better still, disembark at János-hegy, the fourth stop and the highest point (527m) in the hills. From atop the 23.5m-tall **Elizabeth Lookout**, with 101 steps, you can see the Tatra Mountains in Slovakia.

5 Chairlift Down

About 700m to the east of the tower is the **Chairlift** (Libegő; www.bkv.hu; adult/child 900/600Ft; ☾10am-7pm May-Aug, to 6pm Apr & Sep, to 5pm Mar & Oct, to 3.30pm Nov-Feb), which will take you 1040m down at 4km/h to XII Zugligeti út. From here bus 291 will take you to II Szilágyi Erzsébet fasor.

6 Top-Class Dinner

The 291 stops in front of **Szép Ilona** (☎1-275 1392; www.szepilonavendeglo.hu; II Budakeszi út 1-3; mains 1600-3600Ft; ☾noon-11pm; 🚌61), a Buda Hills spot that is the place to come for hearty indigenous fare. But if you'd like something a bit more, well, 21st century, Fióka, a newish bistro and wine bar is almost next to the Cog Railway's lower terminus.

7 Winning Cocktails

Stop for a drink or two at **Oscar American Bar** (☎06 20 214 2525; www.oscarbar.hu; I Ostrom utca 14; ☾5pm-2am Mon-Thu, to 4am Fri & Sat; Ⓜ M2 Széll Kálmán tér) just up from II Széll Kálmán tér on the way up to Castle Hill.

Explore

Belváros

Belváros (Inner Town) is the very heart of Pest and contains the most valuable commercial real estate in the city. The area north of busy Ferenciek tere is full of flashy boutiques, well-frequented bars and restaurants, and tourists. The neighbourhood to the south is somewhat studenty, quieter and more local, but there's no shortage of cafes, along with the usual souvenir shops.

The Sights in a Day

Spend the morning strolling along V **Váci utca** (p64) as far as V **Vörösmarty tér** (p65), taking in the sights and perhaps doing a spot of shopping. For a view of Belváros like no other, hop on a BKV passenger ferry for a brief cruise along the river.

Explore the area around **Egyetem tér** (p68), taking in the wealth of shops in this neighbourhood. Then move toward the Danube. The **Inner Town Parish Church** (p68) is worth a look inside. But even better is the **Pesti Vigadó** (p68); the expansive views of the river from its terrace are sensational.

Round off the day with a coffee at **Gerbeaud** (p65) or for something stronger with even more dramatic vistas head for the **Tip Top Bar** (p70). For dinner with music you couldn't do better than **Kárpátia** (p69). Toward the bewitching hour, head north for V Erzsébet tér and the **Akvárium Klub** (p71). There's no hurry, though; the place raves till well past the break of day.

For a local's day in Belváros, see p64.

Local Life

Exploring Váci utca & Vörösmarty tér (p64)

❤ Best of Budapest

Eating
Kárpátia (p69)

Gepárd És Űrhajó (p69)

Drinking
Gerbeaud (p65)

Akvárium Klub (p71)

Shopping
XD Design & Souvenir (p71)

Getting There

Ⓜ **Metro** M3 Ferenciek tere, M1 Vörösmarty tér, M1/2/3 Deák Ferenc tér, M3/4 Kálvin tér.

🚌 **Bus** Bus 7 or 7E from Buda or points east in Pest to V Ferenciek tere.

🚋 **Tram** Trams 47 or 49 from south Buda along the Little Ring Rd to V Deák Ferenc tér; tram along riverfront Belgrád rakpart.

○ Local Life
Exploring Váci utca & Vörösmarty tér

The total length of Pest in the Middle Ages, **Váci utca** (⊟7, ⓂM1 Vörösmarty tér. M3 Ferenciek tere, ⊟2) is Budapest's premier shopping street and is crammed with chain stores, touristy restaurants and a smattering of shops and notable buildings worth seeking out. It ends at smart **Vörösmarty tér** (ⓂM1 Vörösmarty tér), which contains among other things Gerbeaud, the capital's finest *cukrászda* (cake shop).

❶ Párisi Udvar

Start your tour in Ferenciek tere. Just opposite is **Párisi udvar** (Parisian Court; V Ferenciek tere 5), built in 1909 by Ödön Lechner. It's undergoing a protracted renovation, but try to catch a glimpse of the interior and its ornately decorated ceiling. Váci utca is immediately to the west.

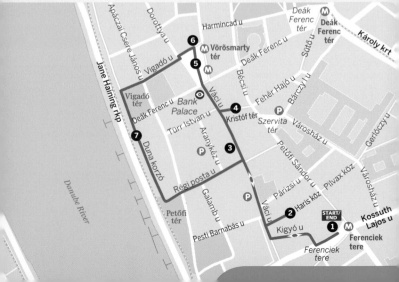

❷ Haris köz Shops

Almost an alleyway, narrow Haris köz contains two traditional shops: **Vass Shoes** (www.vass-cipo.hu; V Haris köz 2; ⏰10am-6pm Mon-Fri, to 2pm Sat; Ⓜ M3 Ferenciek tere), which cobbles men's footwear to order, and **Balogh Kesztyű Üzlet** (V Haris köz 2; ⏰11am-6pm Mon-Thu, to 5pm Fri, to 1pm Sat; Ⓜ M3 Ferenciek tere), with a wide range of custom-made gloves for both men and women.

❸ Art & Architecture

Continue up Váci utca to the **Philanthia flower and gift shop** (V Váci utca 9; 🚇2), which has an original Art Nouveau interior from 1906. **Thonet House** (V Váci utca 11/a; 🚇2), built in 1890, is another Lechner masterpiece and, to the west, at Régi Posta utca 13, there's a relief of an old postal coach by the Szentendre ceramicist Margit Kovács.

❹ Fountain & Palace

Just off the top of Váci utca in Kristóf tér is the 19th-century Fishergirl Fountain, complete with a ship's wheel that actually turns. Further north along Váci utca, the sumptuous **Bank Palace** (Bank Palota; V Deák Ferenc utca 5), built in 1915 and once the home of the Budapest Stock Exchange, now houses a shopping mall.

❺ Vörösmarty tér

Vörösmarty tér (Ⓜ M1 Vörösmarty tér) is a large square of smart shops, galleries, cafes and an artist or two who will draw your portrait or caricature. In the centre is a statue of Mihály Vörösmarty, the 19th-century poet after whom the square is named.

Váci utca shopfronts

❻ Gerbeaud

At the northern end of the square is **Gerbeaud** (📞1-429 9001; www.gerbeaud.hu; V Vörösmarty tér 7; cakes from 1950Ft; ⏰9am-9pm; Ⓜ M1 Vörösmarty tér), Budapest's fanciest and most famous cafe and cake shop. Grab a seat on the terrace and don't fail to order the *Dobos torta*, a scrumptious layered chocolate-and-cream cake with a caramelised brown sugar top.

❼ Duna korzó

A pleasant way to return to Ferenciek tere is along the Duna korzó, the riverside 'Danube Promenade' between Chain and Elizabeth Bridges.

ERZSÉBETVÁROS

BELVÁROS

200 m
0.12 miles

Holló u

Síp u

Dohány u

Rákóczi út

Astoria

Múzeum krt

Gozsdu Udvar

Dob u

Rumbach Sebestyén u

Madách Imre út

Magyar u

Kossuth Lajos u

Szép u

Király u

Asbóth u

Semmelweis u

Vitkovics M u

Várnegye u

Pest
County
Hall

Károly krt

Gerlóczy u

Bajcsy-Zsilinszky út

Deák
Ferenc tér

Városháza

Municipal
Council
Office

Deák
Ferenc
tér

Sütő u

Barczy u

Ferenciek
tere

Fehér Hajó u

Szervita
tér

Petőfi Sándor u

Haris köz

Erzsébet
tér

Budapest
Info main
branch

Bécsi u

Kristóf tér

12

Párizsi u

Hild
tér

Október 6 u

Pesti Barnabás u

József Attila u

Harmincad u

Deák Ferenc u

Vácu

Aranykéz u

11

Galamb u

Nádor u

József
nádor
tér

Vörösmarty
tér

Vörösmarty
tér

Türr István u

Régi posta u

Dorottya u

Vigadó u

Pesti Vigadó

1

Vigadó tér

Duna
korzó

Petőfi
tér

10

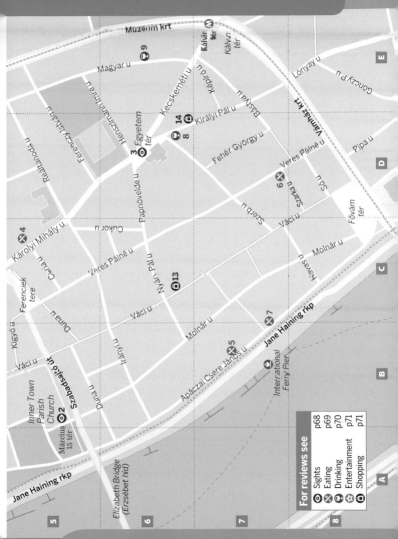

Top Tip

A Different View

A lovely way to see the Belváros from a different angle altogether is to hop on one of the BKV passenger ferries that make stops all along the Danube. Board at IX Boráros tér, from where the ferry crosses to the opposite bank and then returns to Pest; get back on dry land at V Petőfi tér, or stay on for stops up to Margaret Island and beyond.

Sights

Pesti Vigadó   NOTABLE BUILDING

1 💿 Map p66, A3

Pesti Vigadó, the Romantic-style concert hall built in 1864 but badly damaged during WWII, faces the river to the west of Vörösmarty tér. Reopened in 2014 after a 10-year closure and reconstruction, the building has been fully restored to its former grandeur. Additional space has been set aside for temporary exhibitions and there's now a fantastic terrace affording expansive views over the Danube. It's a fantastic place to catch a classical-music concert in the glamorous surrounds.

(www.pestivigado.hu; V Vigadó tér 1; adult/senior 2000/1200Ft, temporary exhibitions 2500Ft; ⏱10am-7.30pm; Ⓜ M1 Vörösmarty tér, 🚋2)

Inner Town Parish Church   CHURCH

2 💿 Map p66, B5

On the eastern side of Március 15 tér, a Romanesque church was first built in the 12th century within a Roman fortress. You can still see bits and pieces of the fort, **Contra Aquincum**, protected under Plexiglas on the square. The present church was rebuilt in the 14th century and again in the 18th century, and you can easily spot Gothic, Renaissance, baroque and even Turkish – eg the *mihrab* (prayer niche) in the eastern wall – elements. (Belvárosi plébániatemplom; www.belvarosiplebania.hu; V Március 15 tér 2; ⏱9am-7pm; 🚋2)

Egyetem tér   SQUARE

3 💿 Map p66, D6

Recently repaved and boasting new lighting, seating, water features and shade sails, 'University Sq' takes its name from the branch of the prestigious **Loránd Eötvös Science University** (ELTE; V Egyetem tér 1-3) located here. Attached to the main university building to the west is the lovely baroque 1742 **University Church** (Egyetemi templom; ☎1-318 0555; V Papnövelde utca 5-7; ⏱7am-7pm; Ⓜ M3 Kálvin tér). Over the altar is a copy of the Black Madonna of Częstochowa so revered in Poland. The building north of the square with the multicoloured dome is the **University Library** (Egyetemi könyvtár; V Ferenciek tere 10).

(University Square; Ⓜ M3/4 Kálvin tér)

Open-air restaurant, Váci utca

Eating

Kárpátia   HUNGARIAN €€€

4 Map p66, C5

A palace of *fin-de-siècle* design dating from 1877 that has to be seen to be believed, the 'Carpathia' serves almost-modern Hungarian and Transylvanian specialities in both a palatial restaurant in the back and a less-expensive *söröző* (brasserie); there's also a lovely covered garden terrace. This is one place to hear authentic *csárdás* (Gypsy-style folk music), played from 6pm to 11pm. (☏1-317 3596; www.karpatia.hu; V Ferenciek tere 7-8; mains 2500-7900Ft; ⏱11am-11pm Mon-Sat, from 5pm Sun; Ⓜ M3 Ferenciek tere)

Gepárd És Űrhajó   HUNGARIAN €€

5 Map p66, B7

It's difficult not to love the 'Cheetah and Rocket', for four reasons: the name, the excellent Hungarian wine (these guys stock more than 100 vintages), the food, and the fabulous river views. In inspired takes on Hungarian dishes such as lamb knuckle or beef cheeks, the meats are cooked to perfection and the weekly specials are based on seasonal ingredients. (☏06 70 329 7815; www.gepardesurhajo. com; V Belgrád rakpart 18; mains 2550-4900Ft; ⏱noon-midnight; Ⓜ M3 Ferenciek tere, ⛴2)

Halkakas
FISH €

6 Map p66, D7

Charming corner restaurant on a quiet street close to Váci utca that throws back its doors on sunny days, when diners spill onto the pavement outside. Fresh, simple and great-value fish dishes are served from the kitchen directly behind the service counter on mismatched plates to happy punters.
(06 30 226 0638; halkakas.hu; V Veres Pálné utca 33; mains 1300-1600Ft; noon-10pm Mon-Sat; M4 Fővám tér)

Local Life
Károly Garden

A glorious place to take a breather is the flora-filled **garden** (Károlyi kert) built for the **Károly Palace**, which houses the **Petőfi Museum of Literature** (Petőfi Irodalmi Múzeum; www.pim.hu; V Károlyi utca 16; adult/child 600/300Ft, plus temporary exhibitions 200/100Ft; 10am-6pm Tue-Sun; 15, 115, M3/4 Kálvin tér). Frequented by locals, many with families – it has a lovely little playground – the garden is a riot of colourful flowerbeds in the summer months, and there are plenty of shady benches. **Csendes Társ** (www.facebook.com/csendestars; Magyar utca 18; 10am-midnight; M2 Astoria, 4, 6) is an atmospheric spot for a sundowner or snack, with a little terrace of tables crowded round the park's pretty, wrought-iron entrance gate.

Trattoria Toscana
ITALIAN €€

7 Map p66, C7

Hard by the Danube, this trattoria serves rustic and very authentic Italian food, including *pasta e fagioli* (soup of beans and pasta) and a Tuscan farmer's platter of prepared meats. The pizza and pasta dishes are excellent, too, as is the antipasto buffet.
(1-327 0045; www.toscana.hu; V Belgrád rakpart 13; mains 2990-5990Ft; noon-midnight; 15, 115, 2)

Drinking

Tip Top Bar
BAR

8 Map p66, D6

The spiral staircase to the 5th floor may be a bit of a hike, but reaching this rooftop bar and relaxing with views out over Egyetem tér and beyond is worth the effort. Call ahead if the weather's bad or you want to secure a table.
(06 70 333 2113; www.facebook.com/pages/Tip-Top-Bar/386238754823394; V Királyi pál utca 4; 4-11pm Apr-Sep; M3/4 Kálvin tér)

Action Bar
GAY

9 Map p66, E6

Action is where to head if you want just that (though there's a strip show at 1am on Friday). Take the usual precautions and don't forget to write home. Men only. Entrance fee includes a drink.
(1-266 9148; www.action.gay.hu; V Magyar utca 42; admission 1000Ft; 9pm-4am; M3/4 Kálvin tér)

Entertainment

Akvárium Klub
LIVE MUSIC

10 ⭐ Map p66, B1

In the old bays below Erzsébet tér you'll now find Akvárium Klub, delivering a varied program of Hungarian and international live music, from indie, jazz, world and pop to electronica and beyond. The main hall has capacity for 1500, the small for 700.
(📞06 30 860 3368; www.akvariumklub.hu; V Erzsébet tér; ⏱ticket office 9am-8pm or end of show Mon-Sat, to 6pm Sun; Ⓜ M1/2/3 Deák Ferenc tér)

Shopping

XD Design & Souvenir
HANDICRAFTS

11 🔒 Map p66, A4

A great place to seek out a modern take on Hungarian handicrafts, XD Design & Souvenir showcases the work of a number of innovative enterprises. Matyo Design preserves the art of embroidery with hand-stitched designs. Great prints, fashion pieces and jewellery also on offer.
(www.facebook.com/pages/XD-DesignSouvenir/1434242860124002; V Régi Posta utca 7-9; ⏱10am-6pm; 🚌2)

Bomo Art
ARTS & CRAFTS

12 🔒 Map p66, B3

This shop just off Váci utca sells some of the finest paper and paper goods in Budapest, including leather-bound notebooks and photo albums.

(www.bomoart.hu; V Régi Posta utca 14; ⏱10am-6.30pm Mon-Fri, to 2pm Sat; Ⓜ M3 Ferenciek tere)

Valeria Fazekas
CLOTHING, HATS

13 🔒 Map p66, C6

Some of the limited headgear in a wide range of colours and fabrics on offer in this small gem of a boutique are out of this world. Artist-designer Fazekas also does silk scarves and stylish tops.
(www.valeriafazekas.com; V Váci utca 50; ⏱10am-6pm Mon-Fri, to 4pm Sat; Ⓜ M3 Ferenciek tere)

Rózsavölgyi Csokoládé
CHOCOLATE

14 🔒 Map p66, D6

Tiny, low-lit boutique selling delicious and artfully packaged, award-winning bean-to-bar chocolate as well as a range of handmade bonbons.
(www.rozsavolgyi.com; V Királyi Pál utca 6; ⏱10.30am-6.30pm Mon-Fri, noon-6pm Sat; Ⓜ M3/4 Kálvin tér)

Explore

Parliament & Around

The district called Lipótváros (Leopold Town) is full of offices, ministries and 19th-century apartment blocks. It's an easy neighbourhood to explore on foot, and home to exceptional architecture, two of the city's most important sights and some excellent restaurants and cafes. When the sun goes down, head east for Terézváros (Theresa Town), a neighbourhood with no shortage of lively watering holes and raving clubs.

The Sights in a Day

Book the first English-language tour at the **Parliament** (p74) building. After your visit and you feel up to it, poke your head into the **Ethnography Museum** (p80) to see how far Hungarian design has come (no judgement) from here to the galleries of Vörösmarty tér.

Have a quick bite at **Pick Ház** (p82) just opposite Parliament and then make your way to **Szabadság tér** (p80), admiring the two Art Nouveau gems nearby: the **Royal Postal Savings Bank** (p80) and the **National Bank of Hungary** (p80). The **Basilica of St Stephen** (p76) is a short distance to the southeast. Visit it on your own or join a tour, and don't forget to make it up to the dome.

After you've finished your pilgrimage, raise a chalice at **DiVino Borbár** (p82). For dinner you couldn't do better than head east to **Pesti Diszno** (p81). Excellent food, more good wine and you will be right on the threshold of the clubs and bars of Terézváros.

👁 Top Sights

Parliament (p74)

Basilica of St Stephen (p76)

♥ Best of Budapest

Eating
Borkonyha (p81)

Pesti Diszno (p81)

Drinking
DiVino Borbár (p82)

Instant (p82)

Getting There

Ⓜ Metro Three stations are close by: Kossuth Lajos tér on the M2, Arany János utca (M3) and Deák Ferenc tér (M1, M2 and M3).

🚌 Bus From Castle Hill bus 16 to V Deák Ferenc tér; from northern Pest bus 15.

🚋 Tram From V Szent István körút or south Pest the waterfront tram 2; from Buda, the 4 or 6 to V Szent István körút.

Top Sights
Parliament

Parliament (Imre Steindl, 1902), an eclectic blend of architectural styles, is Hungary's largest building, counting 691 sumptuously decorated rooms. But you'll only get to see a handful on a guided tour of the North Wing. The choice of location was not made by chance. As a counterweight to the Royal Palace rising high on Buda Hill on the opposite side of the Danube, the placement was meant to signify that the nation's future lay with popular democracy and not royal prerogative.

◉ Map p78, A4

Országház

www.parlament.hu

V Kossuth Lajos tér 1-3

adult/student & EU citizen 4000/2000Ft

Ⓜ M2 Kossuth Lajos tér

Congress Hall, Parliament

Don't Miss

Lion Gate & Ornamental Staircase

The main entrance is through Lion Gate on the eastern side of the building, facing recently renovated V Kossuth Lajos tér. Through this gate you ascend the sweeping 96-step Main Staircase, with frescoes by Károly Lotz and stained glass by Miksa Róth.

Domed Hall & Coronation Regalia

At the top of the stairs you enter the crown-like, 16-sided, 66m-high Domed Hall with statues of Hungary's kings on the capitals. Taking pride of place in the centre is the Coronation Regalia, which includes the Crown of St Stephen, the nation's most important national icon, the 15th-century ceremonial sword, the orb (1301) and the oldest object among the coronation regalia: the 10th-century Persian-made sceptre, with a large crystal head depicting a lion.

Crown of St Stephen

Despite its name, the two-part Crown of St Stephen, with its characteristic bent cross, pendants hanging on either side and enamelled plaques of the Apostles, dates from the 12th century. During WWII it fell into the hands of the US army, which transferred it to Fort Knox in Kentucky. In 1978 the crown was returned to Hungary.

Congress Hall

You'll also visit one of the vaulted anterooms, where political discussions take place, and the 400-seat Congress Hall, where the House of Lords of the one-time bicameral assembly sat until 1944. It is almost identical to the Chamber of the National Assembly, where parliamentary sessions are held, in the South Wing.

☑ **Top Tips**

▶ Opening hours: 8am to 6pm Monday to Friday, and 4pm Saturday and Sunday April to October, and 8am to 4pm daily November to March.

▶ You can join a 45-minute tour in any of eight languages; the English-language ones are at 10am, noon, 1pm, 2pm and 3pm daily. Book ahead in person or online through Jegymester (p136).

▶ There are no tours while the National Assembly is in session.

▶ The ceremonial guards in the Domed Hall change every hour between 8am and 7pm.

✕ **Take a Break**

If you want to try authentic Hungarian sausage or salami but don't feel up to eating at food stalls, you're in the right part of town. Pick Ház (p82), selling Hungary's most celebrated brand of prepared meat, is an eat-in outlet just opposite Parliament.

Top Sights
Basilica of St Stephen

The Basilica of St Stephen is the most important Catholic church in all of Hungary, if for no other reason than that it contains the nation's most revered relic: the mummified right hand of the church's patron. The neoclassical cathedral, the largest in Hungary, is in the form of a Greek cross and can accommodate 8000 worshippers. It was originally designed by József Hild, and though work began in 1851 the structure was not completed until 1905.

Map p78, C7

Szent István Bazilika

www.basilica.hu

V Szent István tér

requested donation 200Ft

M M2 Arany János utca

Interior of Basilica of St Stephen

Don't Miss

Dome
The facade of the basilica is anchored by two large bell towers, one of which contains a bell weighing 9.25 tonnes. Behind the towers is the 96m-high dome, which can be reached by two lifts and 40 steps (or 302 steps if you want to walk). It offers one of the best views in the city.

Interior Decoration
The basilica's interior is rather dark and gloomy, Károly Lotz's shimmering mosaics on the inside of the dome notwithstanding. Noteworthy artwork includes Alajos Stróbl's statue of the king-saint on the main altar and Gyula Benczúr's painting of St Stephen dedicating Hungary to the Virgin Mary, to the right of the main altar.

Holy Right
Behind the altar and to the left is the basilica's major drawcard: the Holy Right Chapel. It contains the Holy Right (also known as the Holy Dexter), the mummified right hand of St Stephen and an object of great devotion.

Treasury
To the right of the basilica's entrance is a small lift to the 2nd-floor treasury of ecclesiastical objects, including censers, chalices, ciboria and vestments. Don't miss the Art Deco double monstrance (1938). Otherwise, the treasury is a veritable shine to Cardinal Mindszenty, including his clothing, devotional objects and death mask.

RICHARD I'ANSON/GETTY IMAGES ©

☑ **Top Tips**

▶ Opening hours: 9am to 5pm April to September, and 10am to 4pm October to March.

▶ English-language guided tours of the basilica (2000/1500Ft with/without dome visit) usually depart at 9.30am, 11am, 2pm and 3.30pm on weekdays and at 9.30am and 11am on Saturday, but phone or check the website to confirm.

▶ Organ concerts are held here at 8pm, usually on Thursday and Friday.

▶ If you want a really good look at the Holy Right put a 200Ft coin in the slot to illuminate the hand for closer inspection. (And view the Holy Right from the right-hand side to see its knuckles.)

✖ **Take a Break**

If it's time for a drink, DiVino Borbár (p82), one of the best wine bars in town, is just opposite.

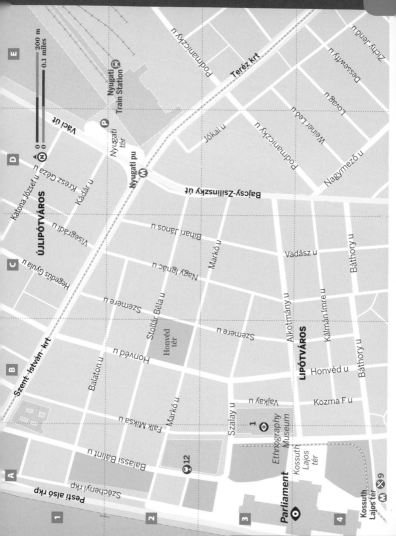

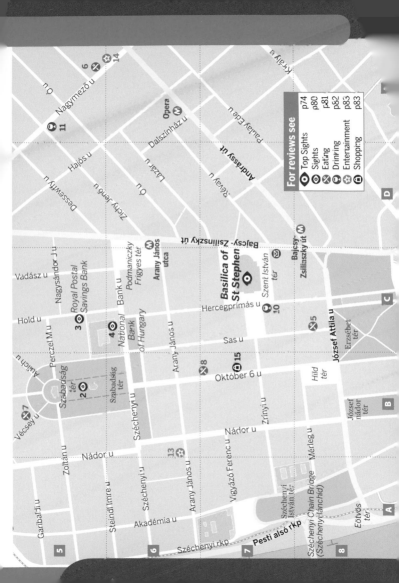

For reviews see

◉ Top Sights	p74
◎ Sights	p80
⊗ Eating	p81
⊗ Drinking	p82
☆ Entertainment	p83
🛍 Shopping	p83

Basilica of St Stephen ◉

Sights

Ethnography Museum   MUSEUM

 1   Map p78, A3

Visitors are offered an easy introduction to traditional Hungarian life at this sprawling museum opposite Parliament. The mock-ups of peasant houses from the Őrség and Sárköz regions of Western and Southern Transdanubia are well done, and there are some priceless objects, which are examined though institutions, beliefs and stages of life.

(Néprajzi Múzeum; ☎1-473 2401; www. neprajz.hu; V Kossuth Lajos tér 12; adult/ concession 1000/500Ft, combined ticket for all exhibitions 1400/700Ft; ⊙10am-6pm Tue-Sun; Ⓜ️M2 Kossuth Lajos tér)

Szabadság tér   SQUARE

2   Map p78, B5

'Liberty Square', one of the largest in Budapest, is a few minutes' walk northeast of Széchenyi István tér. As you enter you'll pass a delightful fountain that works on optical sensors and turns off and on as you approach or back away from it. In the centre of the square is a Soviet army memorial, the last of its type still standing in the city.
(Liberty Square; ☐15)

Royal Postal Savings Bank   NOTABLE BUILDING

3   Map p78, C5

The former Royal Postal Savings Bank is a Secessionist extravaganza of colourful tiles and folk motifs built by Ödön Lechner in 1901.
(V Hold utca 4; ☐15)

National Bank of Hungary   NOTABLE BUILDING

4   Map p78, C6

The National Bank of Hungary has reliefs that illustrate trade and commerce through history: Arab camel traders, African rug merchants, Chinese tea salesmen and the inevitable solicitor witnessing contracts.
(Magyar Nemzeti Bank; V Szabadság tér 9; ☐15)

Understand

Cardinal Mindszenty

In 1948, when Cardinal József Mindszenty (1892–1975) refused to secularise Hungary's Roman Catholic schools under the new Communist regime, he was arrested, tortured and sentenced to life imprisonment for treason. Released during the 1956 Uprising, the cardinal took refuge in the US Embassy when the Communists returned to power. In the late 1960s, the Vatican made several requests for Mindszenty to leave Hungary, which he refused to do so until 1971, when he retired to Vienna.

Royal Postal Savings Bank

KRZYSZTOF DYDYNSKI/GETTY IMAGES ©

Eating

Borkonyha
HUNGARIAN €€€

 5   Map p78, C8

The third restaurant in Budapest to receive a Michelin star well and truly deserves the honour. When we last visited – before said honour was bestowed – we were overwhelmed by the food, the astonishing selection of fine Hungarian wine (200 types, four dozen by the glass) and the warm and knowledgeable service.
(Wine Kitchen; ☑1-266 0835; www. borkonyha.hu; V Sas utca 3; mains 3750-7150Ft; ⏱noon-midnight Mon-Sat; ☑15, MM1 Bajcsy-Zsilinszky út)

Pesti Disznó
HUNGARIAN €€

 6   Map p78, E5

Punters would be forgiven for thinking that the 'Pest Pig' was all about pork. In fact, of the dozen main courses half are poultry, fish or vegetarian. It's a wonderful space, loft-like almost, with high tables and charming, informed service. The wine card is very, very good and most wines are available by the glass, too.
(☑1 951 4061; www.pestidiszno.hu; VI Nagymező utca 19; mains 1490-2890Ft; ⏱11am-midnight Sun-Wed, to 1am Thu-Sat; MM1 Oktogon)

Da Mario
ITALIAN €€

7 Map p78, B5

Da Mario can't put a foot wrong in our book. While the cold platters, soups and meat and fish mains all look good, we stick to the pasta dishes (2000Ft to 3500Ft) and pizzas (1250Ft to 3000Ft).
(☎1-301 0967; www.damario.hu; V Vécsey utca 3; mains 2000-5500Ft; ⏰11am-midnight; 🚏15, Ⓜ️M2 Kossuth Lajos tér)

Kisharang
HUNGARIAN €

8 Map p78, B7

'Little Bell' is an *étkezde* (canteen serving simple Hungarian dishes) that's top of the list with students and staff of the nearby Central European University. *Főzelék* (480Ft to 650Ft), the traditional Hungarian way of preparing vegetables, is always a good bet here.

Top Tip

Top Tip

Lipótváros is a happy hunting ground for fine dining, especially around the area of the Basilica of St Stephen and the **Central European University**. Terézváros, within the Big Ring Rd, is where you want to go for after-dark fun, though there is no shortage of eateries, including a few very-late-night venues. You'll also find VI Nagymező utca, lined with theatres and music halls, and home to the city's largest gay club, **Club AlterEgo** (www.alteregoclub.hu; VI Dessewffy utca 33; 10pm-6am Fri & Sat).

(☎1-269 3861; www.kisharang.hu/; V Október 6 utca 17; mains 590-2350Ft; ⏰11.30am-9pm; 🚏15)

Pick Ház
HUNGARIAN €

9 Map p78, A4

This self-service eatery sits above the famous salami manufacturer's central showroom opposite Parliament. It's convenient for lunch if you're visiting Parliament or any of the sights in the area. The set menu is 870Ft.
(☎1-331 7783; V Kossuth Lajos tér 9; sandwiches & salads from 225Ft, mains 415-800Ft; ⏰6am-7pm Mon-Thu, to 6pm Fri; Ⓜ️M2 Kossuth Lajos tér)

Drinking

DiVino Borbár
WINE BAR

10 Map p78, C7

Central and always heaving, DiVino is Budapest's most popular wine bar and the crowds spilling out into the square in front of the basilica will immediately tell you that. Choose from 120 types of wine produced by some 30 winemakers under the age of 35, but be careful: those 0.1L glasses (650Ft to 2800Ft) go down quickly.
(☎06 70 935 3980; www.divinoborbar.hu; V Szent István tér 3; ⏰4pm-midnight Sun-Wed, to 2am Thu-Sat; Ⓜ️M1 Bajcsy-Zsilinszky út)

Instant
CLUB

11 Map p78, E5

We still love this 'ruin bar' on Pest's most vibrant nightlife strip and so do all our friends. It has six bars on three levels with underground DJs and dance parties. Always heaving. (📞06 30 830 8747; www.instant.co.hu; VI Nagymező utca 38; 🕐4pm-6am Sun-Thu, to 11am Fri & Sat; Ⓜ️M1 Opera)

Szalai Cukrászda   CAFE

12 🍴 Map p78, A2

This humble cake shop in Lipótváros dating back to 1917 probably has the best cherry strudel (380Ft) in the capital. It does apple and *túrós* (cheese curd) ones too. (📞1-269 3210; http://szalaicukraszda.hu/; V Balassi Bálint utca 7; 🕐9am-7pm Wed-Mon; 🚋2)

Entertainment

Aranytíz Cultural Centre   TRADITIONAL MUSIC

13 ⭐ Map p78, B6

At this cultural centre in Lipótváros, the wonderful Kalamajka Táncház has programs from 7pm on Saturday that run till about midnight. Bring the kids in earlier (about 5pm) for a children's version. (Aranytíz Művelődési Központ; 📞1-354 3400; www.aranytiz.hu; V Arany János utca 10; 🕐box office 2-9pm Mon & Wed, 9am-3pm Sat; 🚋15)

Budapest Operetta   OPERA

14 ⭐ Map p78, E6

This theatre presents operettas, which are always a riot, especially campy ones like *The Gypsy Princess* by Imre

Local Life

Antique Rowing

One of our favourite places to while away part or all of a Saturday morning is along V Falk Miksa utca, which is lined with antique and curio shops. Start at the northern end with **BÁV** (Bizományi Kereskedőház és Záloghitel; 📞1-473 0666; www.bav.hu; XIII Szent István körút 3; 🕐10am-6pm Mon-Fri, to 2pm Sat; 🚋4, 6) and end up at the largest of them all: **Pintér Antik** (www.pinterantik.hu; V Falk Miksa utca 10; 🕐10am-6pm Mon-Fri, to 2pm Sat).

Kálmán or Ferenc Lehár's *The Merry Widow*. There's an interesting bronze statue of Kálmán outside the main entrance. (Budapesti Operettszínház; 📞1-312 4866; www.operettszinhaz.hu; VI Nagymező utca 17; tickets 1000-8000Ft; 🕐box office 10am-7pm Mon Fri, 1 7pm Sat & Sun; Ⓜ️M1 Opera)

Shopping

Bestsellers   BOOKS

15 🔒 Map p78, B7

Our favourite English-language bookshop in town, with fiction, travel guides and lots of Hungarica, as well as a large selection of newspapers and magazines overseen by master bookseller Tony Láng. (📞1-312 1295; www.bestsellers.hu; V Október 6 utca 11; 🕐9am-6.30pm Mon-Fri, 10am-5pm Sat, 10am-4pm Sun; Ⓜ️M1/2/3 Deák Ferenc tér)

Explore

Margaret Island & Northern Pest

Neither Buda nor Pest, Margaret Island (Margit-sziget) is not overly endowed with important sights but boasts a couple of large swimming complexes, a thermal spa, gardens and shaded walkways. It's a lovely place to head on a hot afternoon. To the east Újlipótváros (New Leopold Town) is a wonderful neighbourhood with tree-lined streets, boutiques, restaurants and cafes. It too is best seen on foot.

JONATHON SMITH/GETTY IMAGES ©

The Sights in a Day

☀️ Revisit Budapest's medieval past on Margaret Island by strolling or cycling among the ruins of the **Franciscan church and monastery** (p87), one-time **Dominican convent** (p87) where St Margaret is buried and the **Premonstratensian Church** (p87).

☼ There are very few places to eat on the island. Grab some take-away from **Gasztró Hús-Hentesáru** (p90) just over Margaret Bridge in Buda before pampering yourself at the **Danubius Health Spa Margitsziget** (p88), one of the most modern spas in town.

🌙 Pour yourself over the bridge and walk up Pozsonyi út to pay homage to the heroic Raoul Wallenberg at his statue in **Szent István Park** (p88). Have dinner at **Firkász** (p89) and spend the rest of the evening at the incomparable **Budapest Jazz Club** (p91).

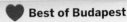

💙 **Best of Budapest**

Eating
Laci Konyha (p89)

Firkász (p89)

Drinking
Holdudvar (p90)

Dunapark (p90)

Entertainment
Budapest Jazz Club (p91)

Thermal Baths & Pools
Danubius Health Spa Margitsziget (p88)

Getting There

🚌 **Bus** Bus 26, running between Nyugati train station and Árpád Bridge, covers the length of Margaret Island. Reach Újlipótváros via bus 15.

🚊 **Tram** Both districts are served by trams 4 and 6. Tram 2 from XIII Jászai Mari tér to Belváros.

Ⓜ **Metro** The eastern end of Újlipótváros is best reached by metro (M3 Nyugati pályaudvar).

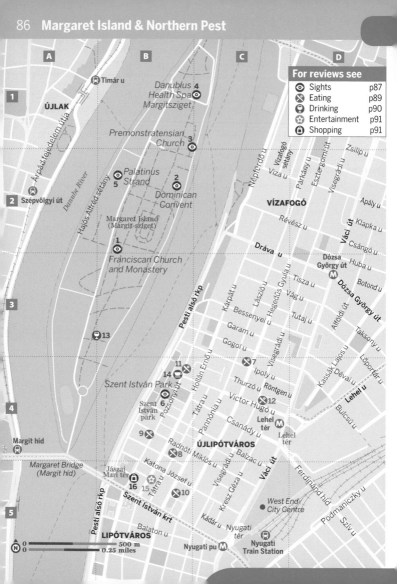

A | B | C | D

For reviews see
⊙	Sights	p87
✖	Eating	p89
🍷	Drinking	p90
✿	Entertainment	p91
🔒	Shopping	p91

Timár u

Danublus **4**
Health Spa
Margitsziget

ÚJLAK

Árpád fejedelem útja

Premonstratensian
Church **3**

Palatinus **5**
Strand

Dominican **2**
Convent

VÍZAFOGÓ

Szépvölgyi út

Hajós Alfréd sétány

Danube River

Margaret Island
(Margit-sziget)

Franciscan Church **1**
and Monastery

Zsilip u

Vízafogó sétány

Népfürdő u

Viza u

Parkány u

Esztergomi út

Visegrádi u

Apály u

Révész u

Váci út

Klapka u

Csángó u

Dráva u

Dózsa
György út **M**

Huba u

Botond u

Dózsa György út

Tisza u

Altföldi út

Taksony u

Kárpát u

László u

Hegedűs Gyula u

Vág u

Tutaj u

Bessenyei u

Kassák Lajos u

Lőportár u

Dévai u

Garam u

Gogol u

Visegrádi u

Lehel u

Pesti alsó rkp

Bulcsú u

13

11 ✖
14 🔒
Szent István Park **6**

Pozsonyi út

7 ✖

Ipoly u

Röntgen u

Thurzó u

Victor Hugó u

12 ✖

Tátra u

Hollán Ernő u

Csanády u

Lehel
tér **M**

Lehel
tér

Szent
István
park

Pannónia u

9 ✖

Radnóti Miklós u

Balzac u

ÚJLIPÓTVÁROS

Váci út

Ferdinánd híd

Margit híd

8 ✖

Margaret Bridge
(Margit híd)

Jászai
Mari tér

Katona József u

Visegrádi u

Kresz Géza u

West End
City Centre

Podmaniczky u

Szív u

16 **15** 🏛

10 ✖

Tátra u

Szent István krt

Pesti alsó rkp

Balaton u

Kádár u

Nyugati
tér

LIPÓTVÁROS

Nyugati pu **M**

Nyugati
Train Station

0 ___ 500 m
0 ___ 0.25 miles

Statue of Raoul Wallenberg by Györfi Sándor, Szent István Park (p88)

Sights

Franciscan Church and Monastery RUIN

1 ⊙ Map p86, B2

The ruins, which date to the late 13th century, are in the centre of the island. Habsburg Archduke Joseph built a summer residence here in 1867. It was later converted into a hotel.
(Ferences templom és kolostor; Margit-sziget; 🚌26)

Dominican Convent RUIN

2 ⊙ Map p86, B2

A ruin is all that remains of the 13th-century convent built by Béla IV, where his daughter, St Margaret (1242–71) lived. According to the story, the king promised to commit his daughter to a life of devotion in a nunnery if the Mongols were driven from the land. They were and she was – at nine years of age. A red-marble sepulchre cover surrounded by a wrought-iron grille marks her original resting place.
(Domonkos kolostor; 🚌26)

Premonstratensian Church CHURCH

3 ⊙ Map p86, B1

This reconstructed Romanesque Premonstratensian Church dedicated to St Michael by the order of

White Canons dates back to the 12th century. The church's 15th-century bell mysteriously appeared one night in 1914 under the roots of a walnut tree knocked over in a storm. It was probably buried by monks during the Turkish invasion.

(Premontre templom; 🚌26)

Danubius Health Spa Margitsziget

SPA

4 Map p86, C1

Among the most modern (but least atmospheric) of all Budapest bathhouses, this thermal spa is in the Danubius Thermal Hotel Margitsziget. The baths are open to men and women in separate sections weekdays and mixed

at the weekend. A daily ticket includes entry to the swimming pools, sauna and steam room, as well as use of the fitness machines.

(📞1-889 4737; www.danubiushotels. com; Mon-Fri 4900Ft, Sat & Sun 5900Ft; ⏰6.30am-9.30pm; 🚌26)

Palatinus Strand

SWIMMING

5 Map p86, B2

The largest series of pools in the capital, the 'Palatinus Beach' complex features upwards of a dozen pools (two of these have thermal water), wave machines, water slides and kids' pools.

(📞1-340 4505; http://en.palatinusstrand. hu; XIII Margit-sziget; adult/child weekday 2600/1900Ft, weekend 3000/1900Ft; ⏰9am-7pm May-Aug; 🚌26)

Szent István Park

PARK

6 Map p86, B4

St Stephen Park contains a **statue of Raoul Wallenberg** doing battle with a snake (evil) that was erected in 1999. It is titled *Kígyóölő* (Serpent Slayer) and replaces one created by sculptor Pál Pátzay that was mysteriously removed the night before its unveiling in 1948. Facing the river you'll see a row of Bauhaus apartments, which were the delight of modernist architecture fans when they were built in the late 1920s.

(Szent István körút; 🚌15, trolleybus75)

Understand

St Margaret's Island

The island's most famous resident was Béla IV's daughter, Margaret. The king supposedly pledged her to a life of devotion in a nunnery if the Mongols, who had overrun Hungary in 1241–42, were expelled. They were and she was – at age nine. Still, she seemed to enjoy it (if we're to believe *Lives of the Saints*), especially the mortification-of-the-flesh parts. Canonised only in 1943, St Margaret commands something of a cult following in Hungary. A red marble sepulchre cover at the site marks her original resting place, and there's a much-visited shrine with votives nearby.

Eating

Laci Konyha
HUNGARIAN €€€

 7 Map p86, C4

One of the most ambitious eateries in Budapest, this self-styled 'boutique restaurant', in the unlikely northern wilds of Újlipótváros, is under the watchful gaze of chef Gábor Mogyorósi who puts a eclectic spin on old favourites (bok choy with guinea fowl, Japanese mushrooms with oxtail). The daily two-course lunch is a snip at 2200Ft. (☎06 70 370 7475; http://lacikonyha.com; Hegedűs Gyula utca 56; mains 3400-4500Ft; ⏱noon-3pm & 6-10pm Mon-Fri; ☐15, Ⓜ M3 Lehel tér)

Firkász
HUNGARIAN €€

 8 Map p86, B4

Set up by former journalists, this retro-style restaurant called 'Hack', with lovely old mementos on the walls, great homestyle cooking, a good wine list and nightly piano music, has been one of our favourite Hungarian 'nostalgia' eateries for years. (☎1-450 1118; www.firkasz.hu; Tátra utca 18; mains 2490-5420Ft; ⏱noon-midnight; ☐15)

Pozsonyi Kisvendéglő
HUNGARIAN €

 9 Map p86, B4

Visit this neighbourhood restaurant on the corner of Pozsonyi út for the ultimate local Budapest experience: gargantuan portions of Hungarian classics (don't expect gourmet), rock-bottom prices and a cast of local char-

Local Life
Wheeling About the Island

Although private motor vehicles are banned, the variety of moving conveyances available for rent on Margaret Island knows no bounds. You can hire a bike from one of several stands on the northern end of the athletic stadium as you walk from Margaret Bridge. Long-established **Bringóhintó** (☎1-329 2073; www.bringohinto.hu; mountain bike per 30/60min 690/990Ft, pedal coach for 4 people per 30/60min 2180/3480Ft; ⏱8am-dusk) rents out all kinds of equipment from the refreshment stand near the Japanese Garden at the northern part of the island. Families love the pedal coaches.

acters. There's a bank of tables on the pavement in summer and a weekday set menu for 950Ft. (☎1-787 4877; www.facebook.com/PozsonyiK isvendeglo?rf=165846513475746; XIII Radnóti Miklós utca 38; mains 1100-2500Ft; ⏱11am-11pm; ☐2, 4, 6, trolleybus75, /6)

Pándzsáb Tandoori
INDIAN €€

 10 Map p86, B5

It may not look like much, but get closer and your olfactories will tell you that this little hole-in-the-wall place with upstairs tables serves some of the best home-cooked Indian food in Budapest. The signature tandoori dishes are excellent, and there's also a good choice of vegetarian dishes.

Top Tip

A Meaty Break

Outside the hotels catering is limited on Margaret Island, so visit **Gasztró Hús-Hentesáru** (1-212 4159; II Margit körút 2; dishes from 300Ft; ⏰7am-6pm Mon, 6am-7pm Tue-Fri, 6am-1pm Sat; 🚋4, 6), a traditional butcher shop opposite the tram stop (4 or 6) on the Buda side of Margaret Bridge also serving cooked sausages and roast chicken to be eaten in situ or taken away.

(☎1-270 2974; http://pandzsabtandoori.blog.hu/; XIII Pannónia utca 3; mains 1560-3800Ft; ⏰noon-11pm; 🍴; 🚋15, 115)

Sarki Fűszeres

CAFE €

11 Map p86, B4

This delightful retro-style cafe on tree-lined Pozsonyi út is the perfect place for brunch, a late breakfast or just a quick sandwich.

(Grocery Store on Corner; ☎1-238 0600; http://sarkifuszeres.hu; Pozsonyi út 53-55; breakfast & sandwiches 750-1900Ft; ⏰8am-8pm Mon-Fri, to 3pm Sat; trolleybus76)

Trófea Grill

BUFFET €€

12 Map p86, C4

This is the place to head when you really could eat a horse (which may or may not be on one of the serving tables). It's an enormous buffet of more than 100 cold and hot dishes over which appreciative diners swarm like bees.

(1-270 0366; www.trofeagrill.hu; XIII Visegrádi utca 50/a; lunch weekdays/weekends 3899/5999Ft, dinner 5499/5999Ft; ⏰noon-midnight Mon-Fri, 11.30am-midnight, 11.30am-8.30pm Sun; 🚋15, Ⓜ M3 Lehel tér)

Drinking

Holdudvar

CLUB

13 🍷 Map p86, A3

Trying to be all things to all people – restaurant, bar, gallery, open-air cinema, disco and *kert* (outdoor garden club) – is not always advisable, but the 'Moon Court', occupying a huge indoor and outdoor space on Margaret Island, does a decent job of juggling all five tasks.

(☎1-236 0155; www.holdudvar.net; XIII Margit-sziget; ⏰11am-midnight Sun-Tue, to 2am Wed, to 4am Thu-Sat; 🚋4 or 6)

Dunapark

CAFE

14 🍷 Map p86, B4

Built in 1938 as a cinema, this Art Deco place with a lovely upstairs gallery and views of Szent István Park is also a restaurant. But we still think of – and use – it as a *cukrászda* (cake shop); its cakes (375Ft to 650Ft) are among the best this side of the Danube.

(☎1-786 1009; www.dunaparkkavehaz.hu; XIII Pozsonyi út 38; ⏰8am-11pm Mon-Fri, 10am-11pm Sat, 10am-10pm Sun; trolleybus 75, 76)

LONELY PLANET/GETTY IMAGES ©

Pozsonyi Kisvendéglő (p89)

Entertainment

Budapest Jazz Club   JAZZ

15 ⭐ Map p86, B5

A very sophisticated venue – now pretty much the most serious one in town – for traditional, vocal and Latin jazz by local and international talent. Concerts most nights at 9pm, with jam sessions at 10pm or 11pm on Friday, Saturday and Monday.
(📱06 70 413 9837; www.bjc.hu; XIII Hollán Ernő utca 7; 🕙10am-midnight; trolleybus 75, 76)

Shopping

Mézes Kuckó   FOOD

16 🅰 Map p86, B5

This hole-in-the-wall is the place to go if you have the urge for something sweet; its nut-and-honey cookies (240Ft per 10 decagrams) are to die for. A colourfully decorated *mézeskalács* (honey cake; 220Ft to 650Ft) in the shape of a heart makes a lovely gift.
(Honey Nook; XIII Jászai Mari tér 4; 🕙10am-6pm Mon-Fri, 9am-1pm Sat; 🚃2, 4, 6)

Explore

Erzsébetváros & the Jewish Quarter

Visitors will focus on two areas of this district with a split personality: the environs of long and stately Andrássy út and the densely packed streets on the western side of Erzsébetváros. There are plenty of museums and notable buildings in the former to occupy your daytime. Andrássy út, traditionally the Jewish area, is where nocturnal Budapest really comes alive nowadays.

The Sights in a Day

☀️ Spend the morning exploring the old Jewish Quarter by following our Erzsébetváros & Jewish Quarter walk on p126. You'll take in both the **Great Synagogue** (p94) and the **Hungarian Jewish Museum** (p95). On the way to Klauzál tér, the heart of this district, have a look at the **Orthodox Synagogue** (p100), almost austere after the flamboyance of the main temple.

☀️ Have lunch at **Kádár** (p102). If Art Nouveau glass and mosaics are your thing, walk south to Dohány utca and hop on trolleybus 74, which will take you almost to the door of the **Miksa Róth Memorial House** (p101). A brief visit will do. Then walk north along Rottenbiller utca to Kodály körönd and **Andrássy út** (p100) and begin your stroll south down that stately boulevard. Depending on the time, you might visit the **House of Terror** (p100) or join a tour of the **Hungarian State Opera House** (p100).

🌙 Have dinner at the **Spinoza Café** (p102), especially if it's Friday and the *klezmer* (Jewish folk) musicians are performing. Otherwise, check out some of the neighbourhood's best bars and clubs by following our guide to a local's evening in Erzsébetváros on p96.

 Top Sights

Great Synagogue (p94)

 Local Life

Bar-Hopping in Erzsébetváros (p96)

💗 **Best of Budapest**

Eating

Klassz (p102)

Macesz Huszár (p103)

Drinking

Lokál (p104)

Doblo (p104)

Shopping

Printa (p106)

Massolit (p106)

Getting There

Ⓜ **Metro** Three metro lines (M1, M2 and M3) converge at Deák Ferenc tér, handy for western Erzsébetváros; Oktogon is on the M1 metro line and Blaha Lujza tér is on the M2 and M4; also useful are the M2 and M4 Astoria and Keleti pályaudvar stations.

🚋 **Tram** Tram 4 or 6 to/from Buda or the rest of the Big Ring Rd in Pest.

Top Sights
Great Synagogue

Budapest's stunning Great Synagogue, with its crenellated red-and-yellow-glazed-brick facade and two enormous Moorish-style towers, is the largest Jewish house of worship in the world outside New York City, seating 3000 worshippers. Built in 1859 according to the designs of Viennese architect Ludwig Förster, the copper-domed Conservative (not Orthodox) synagogue contains both Romantic-style and Moorish architectural elements. It is sometimes called the Dohány utca Synagogue (Dohány utcai zsinagóga) in reference to its location.

⊙Map p98, B8

Nagy zsinagóga

www.dohanystreetsyna-gogue.hu

VII Dohány utca 2

adult/student & child 2850/2000Ft

Ⓜ M2 Astoria

Interior of Great Synagogue

Don't Miss

Rose Window

Because some elements of the synagogue recall Christian churches – including the central rose window with an inscription from the second book of Moses – the synagogue is sometimes referred to as the 'Jewish cathedral'. It was renovated in the 1990s largely due to private donations, including US$5 million from Estée Lauder, who was born in New York to Hungarian Jewish immigrants.

Interior Fittings

Inside, don't miss the decorative carvings on the Ark of the Covenant by National Romantic architect Frigyes Feszl, who also did the wall and ceiling frescoes of multicoloured and gold geometric shapes. Both Franz Liszt and Camille Saint-Saens played the rebuilt 5000-pipe organ dating from 1859. Concerts are held here in summer.

Hungarian Jewish Museum

The Hungarian Jewish Museum, in an annexe of the synagogue, contains objects related to religious and everyday life. Interesting items include 3rd-century Jewish headstones from Roman Pannonia, a vast amount of liturgical items in silver, and a handwritten book of the local Burial Society from the late 18th century. The Holocaust Memorial Room relates the horrifying events of 1944–45.

Holocaust Memorial

In the garden on the synagogue's north side (opposite VII Wesselényi utca 6), the Holocaust Memorial, designed by Imre Varga in 1991, stands over the mass graves of those murdered by the Nazis in 1944–45. On the leaves of the metal 'tree of life' are the family names of some of the hundreds of thousands of victims.

☑ Top Tips

▶ Opening hours: 10am to 6pm Sunday to Thursday, and 4.30pm Friday April to October; reduced hours November to March

▶ A two-hour walking tour (adult/student 6500/5200Ft) of the Jewish Quarter departing from the Great Synagogue at 10:30am Sunday to Friday includes entry to the synagogue and Jewish museum.

▶ A plaque on the exterior south wall of the synagogue notes that Theodore Herzl, the father of modern Zionism, was born at the site in 1860.

▶ The new Jewish Quarter Exhibition near the Holocaust Memorial has interactive displays, video and artefacts documenting life in this quarter before WWII.

✗ Take a Break

Have lunch at the Spinoza Café (p102) or Kádár (p102) or enjoy gorgeous cakes at Fröhlich Cukrászda (p105).

Local Life
Bar-Hopping in Erzsébetváros

Wander along Király utca or down Gozsdu udvar on a Friday night and it can feel like the whole world and his wife are here. Jostling with wide-eyed tourists and hen and stag parties may leave you wondering whether the locals have deserted this area altogether. They haven't – you just need to know where to find them.

❶ Sample a Hungarian Craft Beer

Tiny **Csak a jó sör** (www.csakajosor.hu; VII Kertész utca 42-44; ⏰2-9pm Mon-Sat; Ⓜ️M1 Oktogon, 🚋4, 6) closes early, so it's a good place to start your evening. True to the name, which translates as 'only good beer', the shelves of this tiny shop are stacked high with brown bottles containing an extensive selection of international bottled craft

beer. Another half-dozen are usually on draught.

❷ Check out a Little Local Bar

With your appetite whetted, it's just a short hop to **Kisüzem** (www.facebook.com/Kisuzem; VII Kis Diófa utca 2; ⊙noon-2am Mon-Wed & Sun, to 3am Thu-Sat; 🛜; 🚌4, 6), where relaxed drinkers hang out on the bar's little outside benches. Head inside for another beer or *pálinka* (fruit brandy) and to check out what live music is on the agenda.

❸ Taste Some Hungarian Wine

On bustling Király utca, **Kadarka** (www.facebook.com/kadarkabar; VII Király utca 42; ⊙4pm-midnight; 🛜; M M1 Opera) offers a huge list of Hungarian wines in a modern, sociable bar. Take a table on the street for a spot of people-watching, or settle on a tall bar stool inside and ask for some advice from the ever-helpful servers.

❹ Hang out in a Garden Club

At **Mika Tivadar Mulató** (www.mikativadarmulato.hu; VII Kazinczy utca 47; ⊙5pm-midnight Sun-Wed, to 6am Thu-Sat; 🛜; M M1/2/3 Deák Ferenc tér) just around the corner you'll find a purple-and-gold ground-floor bar and live music in the small downstairs venue. In the fairy-lit garden, take a seat in the boat and enjoy a drink adrift in a sea of chattering locals.

❺ Stroll a Nightlife Street

Just across the road, Madách Imre út is usually packed. Numerous bars line the pedestrian alley, but locals favour **400 Bar** (www.400bar.hu; VII Kazinczy utca 52; ⊙11am-2am Sun-Wed, to 4am Thu-Sat; 🛜; M M1/2/3 Deák Ferenc tér), where you can grab a bite to eat if feeling peckish. Nearby Gozsdu udvar heaves at night with locals and tourists alike.

❻ Listen to Some Live Music

Further south on Madách Imre út is **Telep** (www.facebook.com/TelepGaleria; VII Madách Imre út 8; ⊙noon-2am Mon-Fri, from 4pm Sat; 🛜; M M1/2/3 Deák Ferenc tér), an exhibition space and art gallery, wallpapered with stickers and hosting nightly live music or DJs. If the weather's warm, the street will be filled with folk hanging out on the pavement with a beer.

❼ Head to a Club

If you're ready to ramp things up a bit, head back towards Gozsdu udvar, where the basement club at **GMK** (Gozsdu Manó Klub; www.gozsdumano.hu; cnr Madách Imre út & Gozsdu udvar; ⊙4pm-2am Mon-Wed & Sun, to 5am Thu-Sat; 🛜; M M1/2/3 Deák Ferenc tér) has an excellent sound system and a good reputation for quality DJs and live music.

ERZSÉBETVÁROS

For reviews see

⊙	Top Sights	p94
⊙	Sights	p100
✕	Eating	p102
🍷	Drinking	p103
🎭	Entertainment	p106
🛍	Shopping	p106

400 m
0.2 miles

Lendvay u
Munkácsy Mihály u
Bajza u
Bajza utca Ⓜ
Bajza u
Szondi u
Bajza u
Benczúr u
Városligeti fasor
Lövölde tér
Jósika u
Székely Bertalan u
Szinyei Merse u
Kmetty György u
Aradi u
Felső erdősor
Rottenbiller u
Rózsa u
Izabella u
Király u
Szófia u
Kodály körönd Ⓜ
Kodály körönd
Szinyei Merse u
Bajnok u
Szív u
Aradi u
Andrássy út
Andrássy út
⊙1
✦27
⊙6
Ferenc Liszt
Memorial Museum
Hunyadi tér
Csengery u
Rózsa u
Izabella u
Vörösmarty utca Ⓜ
Vörösmarty
utca
House of
Terror
⊙3
Eötvös u
Podmaniczky u
Szondi u
Vörösmarty u
Csengery u
Eötvös u
Oktogon Ⓜ Oktogon
ⓘ Budapest
Info
Ferdinánd híd
TERÉZVÁROS
Jókai
tér
12 ✕
Mozsár u
Jókai u
Nagy
Ⓟ
Szobi u
Teréz krt
Teréz krt
Jókai u
Jókai u
Zichy Jenő u
Dessewffy u
Nyugati
Train Station
Ⓚ
Podmaniczky u
Weiner L u
Lovag u
Zichy Jenő u
Nagymező u
Hajó
Ⓟ
Nyugati
tér
Ⓜ Nyugati pu
Jókai u
Bajcsy-Zsilinszky út

Hevesi Sándor tér

Szövetség u

Szövetség u

Kiss József u

Bezerédj u

Vig u

Népszínház u

Vig u

Rákóczi út

Hársfa u

Dohány u

Almássy u

Wesselényi u

Osvát u

Almássy tér

Blaha Lujza tér

József krt

M Blaha Lujza tér

Dob u

Vörösmarty u

Csengery u

Barcsay u

Erzsébet krt

Blaha Lujza tér

Somogyi B u

Hársfa u

Kertész u

Dohány u

JÓZSEFVÁROS

Stáhly u

Erzsébet krt

P

Dob u

Akácfa u

Klauzál u

Vas u

Kürt u

Kertész u

18

Kertész u

ERZSÉBETVÁROS

Wesselényi u

Nyár u

24

Rákóczi út

Szentkirályi u

Liszt Ferenc tér

25

P

Nagy Diófa u

10

11

14

Hegedű u

Csányi u

Klauzál tér

30

Kazinczy u

15

8

19

Kis Diófa u

Ortodox Synagogue

Síp u

Dohány u

20

13

4

Great Synagogue

21

23

17

Holló u

16

9

New Theatre

Paulay Ede u

29

Gozsdu udvar

Dob u

M Astoria

Opera

Madách Imre út

Király u

7

Rumbach S u

28

Hungarian State Opera House

2

Dalszínház u

Andrássy út

Székely Mihály u

Vármegye u

Mérleg u

Semmelweis u

Révay u

Lázár u

Károly krt

Asbóth u

Kálmán Gyula u

26

Gerlóczy u

Kammermayer Károly tér

Arany János utca

M Bajcsy-Zsilinszky út

Bajcsy-Zsilinszky út

22

Deák Ferenc tér

BELVÁROS

5

6

7

8

A

B

C

D

E

Sights

Andrássy út   STREET

1 Map p98, D3

Andrássy út starts a short distance northeast of Deák Ferenc tér and stretches for 2.5km, ending at Heroes' Sq (Hősök tere) and the sprawling City Park (Városliget). On Unesco's World Heritage list, it is a tree-lined parade of knock-out architecture and is best enjoyed as a long stroll from the Opera House out to the park.
(Ⓜ M1 Opera)

Hungarian State Opera House   NOTABLE BUILDING

2 Map p98, B5

The neo-Renaissance Hungarian State Opera House was designed by Miklós

---

☑️ Top Tip

The Right Way to Go

The M1 metro, also known as the Kis Metró (Little Metro), which runs just below Andrássy út from Deák Ferenc tér as far as City Park, sticks to its side of the road underground and there is no interchange down below. If heading north, board the trains on the east side of Andrássy út. For points south, it's the west side. Another possible source of confusion on the M1 is that one station is called Vörösmarty tér and another, five stops away, Vörösmarty utca.

Ybl in 1884 and is among the city's most beautiful buildings. Its facade is decorated with statues of muses and opera greats such as Puccini and Mozart, while its interior dazzles with marble columns, gilded vaulted ceilings and chandeliers, and superb acoustics. If you cannot attend a performance, join one of the tours. Tickets are available from the souvenir shop.
(Magyar Állami Operaház; www.operavisit. hu; VI Andrássy út 22; tours adult/concession 2900/1900Ft; ⏱tours 3pm & 4pm; Ⓜ M1 Opera)

House of Terror   MUSEUM

3 Map p98, C3

The headquarters of the dreaded secret police have been turned into the striking House of Terror, an engrossing and evocative museum focusing on the crimes and atrocities of Hungary's fascist and Stalinist regimes. The years leading up to the 1956 Uprising get the lion's share of the exhibition space. The reconstructed prison cells in the basement and the Perpetrators' Gallery, featuring photographs of the turncoats, spies and torturers, are chilling.
(Terror Háza; www.terrorhaza.hu; VI Andrássy út 60; adult/concession 2000/1000Ft; ⏱10am-6pm Tue-Sun; Ⓜ M1 Oktogon)

Orthodox Synagogue   SYNAGOGUE

4 Map p98, C7

Once one of a half dozen synagogues and prayer houses in the Jewish Quarter, the Orthodox Synagogue was built in 1913 to a very modern – at the time – design. It has late Art Nouveau

Hungarian State Opera House

touches and is decorated in bright colours throughout. The stained-glass windows in the ceiling were designed by Miksa Roth, although what you see today are reconstructions as the originals were bombed during WWII. (Ortodox zsinagóga; VII Kazinczy utca 29-31; admission 1000Ft; ⏰10am-5.30pm Sun-Thu, to 12.30pm Fri; MM2 Astoria, 🚋47, 49)

Miksa Róth Memorial House
MUSEUM

5 ⊙ Map p98, E6

This fabulous museum exhibits the work of the eponymous Art Nouveau stained-glass maker (1865–1944) on two floors of the house and workshop where he lived and worked from 1911 until his death. The master's stunning mosaics are less well known. Róth's dark-brown living quarters stand in sharp contrast to the lively, Technicolor creations that emerged from his workshop. (Róth Miksa Emlékház; www.facebook.com/ rothmiksaemlekhaz; VII Nefelejcs utca 26; adult/child 750/375Ft; ⏰2-6pm Tue-Sun; MM2/4 Keleti pályaudvar)

Ferenc Liszt Memorial Museum
MUSEUM

6 ⊙ Map p98, D3

This wonderful little museum is housed in the Old Music Academy, where the great composer lived in a 1st-floor apartment for five years until his death in 1886. The four rooms are filled with

SPACES IMAGES/GETTY IMAGES ©

his pianos (including a tiny glass one), portraits and personal effects. Concerts (included in the entry fee) are usually held here on Saturday at 11am.
(Liszt Ferenc Emlékmúzeum; www.lisztmuseum.hu; VI Vörösmarty utca 35; adult/child 1300/600Ft; ⏰10am-6pm Mon-Fri, 9am-5pm Sat; Ⓜ M1 Vörösmarty utca)

New Theatre
NOTABLE BUILDING

 Map p98, B5

The New Theatre is a Secessionist gem – embellished with monkey faces, globes and geometric designs – which opened as the Parisiana music hall in 1909. It's worth having a peek inside, too.
(Új Színház; www.ujszinhaz.hu; VI Paulay Ede utca 35; Ⓜ M1 Opera)

Eating

Klassz
INTERNATIONAL €€

 Map p98, B5

Owned by the local wine society, Klassz is mostly about wine – Hungarian, to be precise – and here you can order by the 10cL measure from an ever-changing list of up to four dozen wines

Local Life
Foodie Magnet

Join the foodies getting their artisan produce at the **Szimpla Farmers' Market** (szimpla.hu/szimpla-market; VII Kazinczy utca 14; ⏰9am-2pm Sun; 🛜; Ⓜ M2 Astoria), held every Sunday at Budapest's original 'ruin pub'.

to sip and compare. The food is of a very high standard. Reservations are not accepted; just show up and wait.
(www.klasszetterem.hu; VI Andrássy út 41; mains 1890-5490Ft; ⏰11.30am-11pm; Ⓜ M1 Oktogon)

Spinoza Café
HUNGARIAN €€

 Map p98, B7

This attractive cafe-restaurant includes an art gallery and theatre, where *klezmer* (traditional Jewish music) concerts are staged at 7pm on Friday, along with a coffee house and restaurant where there's live piano music nightly. The food is mostly Hungarian/Jewish comfort food, not kosher but no pork. The €5 breakfast is a steal.
(📞1-413 7488; www.spinozacafe.hu; VII Dob utca 15; mains 1850-4350Ft; ⏰8am-midnight; Ⓜ M2 Astoria)

Kádár
HUNGARIAN €

 Map p98, C6

Located in the heart of the Jewish district, Kádár is probably the most popular and authentic *étkezde* (small restaurant) you'll find in town and it attracts the hungry with its ever-changing menu. Be advised that it usually closes for most of the month of July.
(📞1-321 3622; X Klauzál tér 9; mains 1250-2500Ft; ⏰11.30am-3.30pm Tue-Sat; 🚋4, 6)

Kis Parázs
THAI €

11 Map p98, C7

The sister eatery of **Parázs Presszó** (📞1-950 3770; www.parazspresszo.com; VI Jókai utca 8; mains 1950-2750Ft; ⏰11am-midnight Mon-Fri, from noon Sat & Sun; Ⓜ M1

Oktogon, 🚋4, 6), with simpler dishes, has become a pre-club chow-down venue of choice in central Pest. (☎06 70 517 4550, www.parazspresszo.com; VII Kazinczy utca 7; soup 680-1350Ft, wok dishes 1580-1980Ft; ⊙noon-10pm; ⓂM2 Astoria)

Szimpla Farmers' Cafe CAFE €

Sourcing its ingredients from the farmers selling their wares at the Sunday market (see 11 ✗ Map p98, C7) across the road, this lovely, rustic cafe has a daily menu using seasonal ingredients (soup and a main course for 1100Ft), sandwiches (490Ft), pastries, fresh fruit juices and Has Bean coffee. (szimpla.hu/szimpla-farm-shop; VII Kazinczy utca 7; daily menu 1100Ft; ⊙8am-10pm; 🖍; ⓂM2 Astoria)

bigfish FISH €€

12 ✗ Map p98, B4

Select your type and cooking method at the glass counter, choose a side, and then sit back and wait for superfresh fish and shellfish to be delivered to your table. This simply decorated restaurant has plenty of tables inside, as well as along busy Andrássy út. And there are bibs for you messy eaters. Pasta and rice dishes also available. (☎1-269 0693; www.facebook.com/the-bigfish.hu; VI Andrássy út 44; fish market prices, sides 570Ft, other mains 890-3890Ft; ⊙noon-10pm; ⓂM1 Oktogon)

Macesz Huszár JEWISH, HUNGARIAN €€

13 ✗ Map p98, B7

A wonderful marriage of modern and traditional, the Macesz Huszár serves up Hungarian Jewish dishes in a bistro-style dining room, handsomely dressed up with lace tablecloths, flock wallpaper and rocking horses. The Jewish-style eggs and matzo-ball soup are standout starters; goose and duck feature heavily on the list of mains. (☎1-787 6164; www.maceszhuszar.hu; VII Dob utca 26; mains 1990-5190Ft; ⊙11.30am-midnight)

Menza HUNGARIAN €€

14 ✗ Map p98, C5

This stylish restaurant takes its name from the Hungarian for a drab school canteen – something it is anything but. It's always packed with diners, who come for its simple but well-prepared Hungarian classics with a modern twist, in mid-century-styled dining rooms. Weekday two-course set lunches are 1090Ft; reservations recommended. (☎1-413 1482; www.menzaetterem.hu; VI Liszt Ferenc tér 2; mains 2390-4690Ft; ⓂM1 Oktogon)

Drinking

Szimpla Kert RUIN PUB

15 🍺 Map p98, C7

Budapest's first *romkocsma* (ruin pub), Szimpla Kert is firmly on the drinking-tourists' trail but remains a landmark place for a drink. It's a huge building with nooks filled with bric-a-brac, grafitti, art and all manner of unexpected items. Sit in an old Trabant, watch open-air cinema, down shots or join in an acoustic jam session.

(www.szimpla.hu; VII Kazinczy utca 14; ☻noon-3am; Ⓜ M2 Astoria)

Lokál
RUIN PUB

16 Map p98, B7

A convivial ruin pub offering a variety of distractions – from the escape game in the basement to a tattoo parlour. The less adventurous can rifle through its fancy-dress shop or enjoy a drink in the garden.

(lokalbar.hu; VII Dob utca 18; ☻5pm-midnight Mon-Wed, to 4am Thu-Sat; Ⓜ M1/2/3 Deák Ferenc tér)

Doblo
WINE BAR

17 Map p98, B7

Brick lined and candlelit, Doblo is where you go to taste Hungarian wines, with scores available by the 1.5cL glass for 800Ft to 1650Ft. There's salads, sandwiches and mixed platters of meat or cheese.

(www.budapestwine.com; VII Dob utca 20; ☻10am-2am Mon-Fri, 5pm-3am Sat, 5pm-1am Sun; Ⓜ M1/2/3 Deák Ferenc tér)

La Bodeguita del Medio
BAR

18 Map p98, C6

Anchor tenant of the Fészek Club, meeting place of artists and intellectu-

als since 1901, La Bodeguita del Medio is a Cuban restaurant whose major draw is the city's most beautiful courtyard, filled with trees and surrounded by tiled galleries.

(www.labodeguitadelmedio.hu; VII Dob utca 55; ☻11am-1am Mon-Thu & Sun, to 3am Fri & Sat; 🚊4, 6)

Alexandra Book Cafe
CAFE

19 Map p98, B5

Inside one of Budapest's best bookshops, this glitzy cafe in the revamped Ceremonial Hall shows off Károly Lotz frescoes and other wonderful touches of opulence. Great spot for a light lunch or coffee pre- or post-browse.

(www.parisi.hu; VI Andrassy út 39; ☻10am-10pm; Ⓜ M1 Opera, 🚊4, 6)

Café Zsivágó
CAFE, BAR

20 Map p98, B5

A little Russian living room with lace tablecloths, wooden dressers, mismatched tea sets, hat stands and vintage lamps provides a relaxing daytime coffee stop that morphs into a jumping bar at night offering cocktails, champagne and vodka. If you can, bag the little alcove upstairs.

(cafezsivago.hu; VI Paulay Ede utca 55; ☻10am-midnight Mon-Fri, from noon Sat, 2-10pm Sun; Ⓜ M1 Oktogon, 🚊4, 6)

Művész Kávéház
CAFE

21 Map p98, B5

The Artist Coffeehouse is an interesting place to people watch, though some

Menza (p103)

say its cakes are not what they used to be (though presumably they're not thinking as far back as 1898, when the cafe opened).

(Artist Cafe; www.muveszkavehaz.hu; VI Andrássy út 29; cakes 690-890Ft; 9am-10pm Mon-Sat, 10am-10pm Sun; Ⓜ M1 Opera)

Anker Klub   CLUB

22 🚇 Map p98, A7

A cafe that turns into hipster hangout in the evening, the Anker is spacious and minimalist and about as central as you'll find.

(ankerklub.hu; VI Anker köz 1-3; 11am-4am; Ⓜ M1/2/3 Deák Ferenc tér)

Fröhlich Cukrászda   CAFE

23 🚇 Map p98, B7

This kosher cake shop and cafe in the former ghetto makes and sells old Jewish favourites (230Ft to 450Ft) such as *flódni* (a three-layer cake with apple, walnut and poppy-seed fillings). (www.frohlich.hu; VII Dob utca 22; 9am-6pm Mon-Thu, to 2pm Fri, 10am-6pm Sun; Ⓜ M1/2/3 Deák Ferenc tér)

CoXx Men's Bar   GAY

24 🚇 Map p98, C7

Probably the cruisiest gayme in town, this place with the in-your-face name has 400 sq metres of hunting ground, three bars and some significant play areas in back. Don't bring sunglasses.

(www.coxx.hu; VII Dohány utca 38; ⏱9pm-4am Sun-Thu, to 5am Fri & Sat; Ⓜ M2 Blaha Lujza tér, 🚊4, 6)

Entertainment

Liszt Academy
CLASSICAL MUSIC

25 Map p98, C5

Budapest's most important concert hall has recently emerged from extensive renovations and is looking more fantastic than ever. Performances are usually booked up at least a week in advance, but (expensive) last-minute tickets can sometimes be available – it's always worth checking.
(Liszt Zeneakadémia; 📞1-321 0690; www.zeneakademia.hu; VI Liszt Ferenc tér 8; ⏱ticket office 11am-6pm; Ⓜ M1 Oktogon)

Gödör
LIVE MUSIC

26 ⭐ Map p98, A7

Gödör has a reputation for scheduling an excellent variety of indie, rock, jazz, electronic and experimental music, as well as hosting quality club nights in its spare, industrial space.
(www.godorklub.hu; VII Király utca 8-10; 📶; Ⓜ M1/2/3 Deák Ferenc tér)

Budapest Puppet Theatre
THEATRE

27 ⭐ Map p98, D3

The city's puppet theatre presents a variety of shows for children.
(Budapest Bábszínház; 📞bookings 1-342 2702; www.budapest-babszinhaz.hu; VI Andrássy út 69; 👶; Ⓜ M1 Vörösmarty utca)

Shopping

Printa
CRAFT, CLOTHING

28 Map p98, B7

This wonderful, hip silkscreen studio, design shop and gallery focuses on local talent: bags, leather goods, prints, T-shirts, stationery and jewellery. Also serves great (Has Bean) coffee.
(www.printa.hu; VII Rumbach Sebestyén utca 10; ⏱11am-7pm Mon-Fri, noon-6pm Sat; Ⓜ M1/2/3 Deák Ferenc tér)

Gouba
MARKET

29 Map p98, B7

Weekly arts and crafts market lining Gozsdu udvar, where you can pick up some interesting pieces from local artists and designers. A great place to shop for souvenirs.
(www.gouba.hu; VII Gozsdu udvar; ⏱10am-7pm Sun; Ⓜ M1/2/3 Deák Ferenc tér)

Massolit
BOOKS

30 🔒 Map p98, C7

Branch of the celebrated bookshop in Kraków, Poland, Massolit is one of Budapest's best, with new and secondhand English-language fiction and nonfiction, including Hungarian history and literature in translation. It has a beautiful shady garden and tables set amongst the shelves, so you can enjoy coffee, sandwiches, cakes and bagels as you browse the volumes.
(www.facebook.com/MassolitBudapest; VII Nagy Diófa utca 30; ⏱10am-8pm Mon-Sat, from noon Sun; 📶; Ⓜ M2 Astoria)

Understand

The Jews of Budapest

Jews can trace their presence in Hungary and the area that is now Budapest to at least the 3rd century AD – well before the arrival of the Magyars. Over the centuries, Jews underwent the usual roller-coaster ride of toleration and oppression. They were blamed for the plague and expelled by King Louis the Great (Nagy Lajos) in 1360, but then they were readmitted and prospered under good King Matthias Corvinus and even the Ottoman Turks. With full emancipation after the 1867 Compromise, Jews dominated the burgeoning middle class during Budapest's Golden Age at the end of the 19th century.

After the failure of the communist Republic of Councils under Béla Kun (himself a Jew) in 1919, Miklós Horthy launched his 'white terror' and Jews again became the scapegoats. Life was not easy for Jews under Horthy between the wars, but they were not deported to Germany. But when Hitler removed Horthy from power and installed the Hungarian pro-Nazi Arrow Cross Party, deportations began. During the summer of 1944, a mere 10 months before the war ended, 60% of Hungarian Jews were sent to Auschwitz and other labour camps, where they were murdered or died from abuse.

Jewish contribution to life here, always great, has continued into the 21st century, and the music scene is particularly lively in Budapest. Several restaurants serve kosher food, even more serve non-kosher Jewish dishes, and there are four active synagogues. Today Hungary's Jews (not necessarily claiming to be religious) number about 80,000, down from a prewar population of more than 10 times that. Almost 90% live in Budapest.

But while there has been a revival of Jewish culture in Budapest, there has also been a resurgence of openly expressed anti-Semitism. In November 2012, Márton Gyöngyösi, an MP for the far-right Jobbik party, called for the government to compile a national list of Hungarian Jews, whom he described as a 'national security risk' for alleged solidarity with Israel. Despite the outrage caused by this remark, the party's stances remain popular with voters. Jobbik polled 20% of the vote in the April 2014 parliamentary election.

Explore

Southern Pest

Southern Budapest incorporates two distinct neighbourhoods: Józsefváros (Joseph Town) in district VIII and Ferencváros (Francis Town) in district IX. Once considered rough-and-tumble areas, both are ever-changing and developing, with new shops, bars and restaurants popping up everywhere. Some quarters still feel slightly less salubrious than other places in the city, but they're full of interesting spots.

DE AGOSTINI/G.VANNINI/GETTY IMAGES ©

The Sights in a Day

Begin the day wandering the backstreets between the **Nagycsarnok** (p112) and **Rákóczi tér market** (p113). Then spend an hour or two in the **Hungarian National Museum** (p110); the exhibits relating to the 1956 Uprising will help put what you've seen on your walk into perspective.

In the afternoon, ogle the spectacular Art Nouveau tiles and furniture at the **Museum of Applied Arts** (p115). Carry on to the **Holocaust Memorial Center** (p116). If you're lucky there will be a temporary exhibition in the courtyard's lovingly restored synagogue.

Have a stuff drink at **Élesztő** (p117) and contemplate the evening's possibilities. A curry or thali at **Curry House** (p117) makes for a nice change after all that pork and paprika. Spend the rest of the night grooving at **Corvintető** (p117), one of our favourite Budapest clubs.

For a local's day in Southern Pest, see p112.

Top Sights

Hungarian National Museum (p110)

Local Life

From Market to Market (p112)

Best of Budapest

Eating

Múzeum (p116)

Rosenstein (p116)

Drinking

Élesztő (p117)

Corvintető (p117)

Museums & Galleries

Museum of Applied Arts (p115)

Ludwig Museum of Contemporary Art (p115)

Getting There

Ⓜ **Metro** Key stations include Blaha Lujza tér and Keleti pályaudvar on the M2, Corvin-negyed on the M3, Rákóczi tér on the M4, and Kálvin tér, where the M3 and M4 intersect.

🚋 **Tram** Both districts are served by trams 47 and 49, and further east by trams 4 and 6.

Top Sights
Hungarian National Museum

The Hungarian National Museum houses the nation's most important collection of historical relics. It traces the history of the Carpathian Basin and that of the Magyar people and their nation from the 9th-century conquest to the end of communism. The museum was founded in 1802 when Count Ferenc Széchényi donated his personal collection of more than 20,000 prints, maps, manuscripts, coins and archaeological finds to the state. It is housed in an impressive neoclassical edifice, purpose built by Mihály Pollack in 1847.

👁 Map p114, B2

Magyar Nemzeti Múzeum

www.hnm.hu

VIII Múzeum körút 14-16

adult/concession 1600/800Ft

🚌47, 49, Ⓜ M3/4 Kálvin tér

Facade of Hungarian National Museum

Don't Miss

Front Steps

Less than a year after it moved into its new premises, the museum was the scene of a momentous event (though, as is often the case, this wasn't recognised as such at the time). On 15 March a crowd gathered to hear the poet Sándor Petőfi recite his 'Nemzeti Dal' (National Song) from the front steps, sparking the 1848–49 revolution.

Archaeological Exhibition

Exhibits on the 1st floor trace the history of the Carpathian Basin and its peoples from earliest times to the end of the Avar period in the early 9th century. Don't miss the Golden Stag, a hand-forged Iron Age figure from the 6th century BC once part of a Scythian prince's shield. At the entrance is a stunning 2nd-century Roman mosaic from Balácapuszta, near Veszprém.

Coronation Mantle

In its own room on the 1st floor, you'll find King Stephen's beautiful crimson silk coronation mantle, stitched by nuns in 1031. It was refashioned in the 13th century and the much faded cloth features an intricate embroidery of fine gold thread and pearls.

Museum Gardens

You may enjoy walking around the museum gardens, laid out in 1856. The Roman column to the left of the museum entrance once stood at the Forum and was a gift from Mussolini. Among the monuments is a statue of János Arany (1817–82), author of the epic *Toldi Trilogy*.

JEAN-PIERRE LESCOURRET/GETTY IMAGES ©

☑ Top Tips

▶ Opening hours: 10am to 6pm Tuesday to Sunday

▶ Audioguides to the permanent collection are available in English for 750Ft.

▶ The museum shop sells excellent reproductions of 3rd-century Celtic gold and silver jewellery.

▶ Should you be in the area on National Day (15 March), expect a lot of pomp and circumstance as Petőfi's reading of his 'National Song' is re-enacted on the museum's front steps.

✕ Take a Break

The excellent and very attractive Építész Pince (p116) is literally at the back door, but if you just want a drink, head east to Mikszáth Kálmán tér and Lumen (p117) for some of the best coffee and local craft beers in town.

Local Life
From Market to Market

The ideal way to appreciate these two fascinating but large traditionally working-class districts is to pick a sight and then spend some time wandering in the nearby streets. We've chosen an area between two great markets that is filled with antiquarian bookshops, ghosts from the 1956 Uprising, unusual architecture and trendy bars and restaurants.

① Nagycsarnok

The **Nagycsarnok** (Great Market; www.piaconline.hu; IX Vámház körút 1-3; ⊙6am-5pm Mon-Fri, to 3pm Sat; ⓂM4 Fővám tér) is Budapest's largest market. Though it has become a tourist magnet since its renovation for the millecentenary celebrations in 1996, plenty of locals come here for fruit, vegetables, deli items, fish and meat. Head up to the 1st floor for Hungarian

folk costumes, dolls, painted eggs, embroidered tablecloths, carved hunting knives and other souvenirs.

❷ Breaking for Brunch

Ráday utca, a long strip where pavement tables fill with diners on warm summer days, is a lively place to head to in this district at any time of day. Stop for brunch at **Jedermann** (www. jedermannkavezo.blogspot.com; XI Ráday utca 58; ☺8am-1am; 🛜; 🚊4, 6), an über-chilled cafe and restaurant at the southern end of the street.

❸ Antiquarian Bookshop

The western side of Múzeum körút is lined with shops selling antiquarian and secondhand books. Our favourite is **Múzeum Antikvárium** (www. muzeumantikvarium.hu; V Múzeum körút 35; ☺10am-6pm Mon-Fri, to 2pm Sat; Ⓜ M3/4 Kálvin tér) just opposite the Hungarian National Museum. Further north is **Központi Antikvárium** (V Múzeum körút 13-15; ☺10am-6pm Mon-Fri, 10am-2pm Sat), the largest in town.

❹ Brody House

Now a fancy-schmancy hotel, Brody House would have lots of tales to tell could it speak. It was the residence of Hungary's prime minister in the 19th century when Parliament sat next door at No 8. And if you don't believe that, look at the verso of the 20,000Ft note.

❺ Former Hungarian Radio Headquarters

On the evening of 23 October 1956 ÁVH government agents fired on a group of protesters gathering outside these **radio headquarters** (Magyar Rádió; VIII Bródy Sándor utca 5-7) when they began shouting anti-Soviet slogans and demanding that reformist Imre Nagy be named prime minister. By morning Budapest was in revolution.

❻ Rákóczi tér Market

Rákóczi tér has sported this handsome and very authentic **market hall** (www. piaconline.hu; VIII Rákóczi tér 7-9; ☺6am-4pm Mon, to 6pm Tue-Fri, to 1pm Sat; Ⓜ M4 Rákóczi tér, 🚊4, 6) since 1897. Inside you'll find all the usual staples – fruit, veg, cured meats, cheese, jam and baked goods – and some folk bring their goods up direct from the farm.

❼ Coffee at the 'Snail'

Finish off your day at **Café Csiga** (www. facebook.com/cafecsiga; VIII Vásár utca 2; ☺10am-midnight; 🛜; Ⓜ M4 Rákóczi tér, 🚊4, 6), a relaxed space just opposite the market, with battered wooden floorboards, copious plants and wide-open doors on sunny days. The Snail does food, too, including lots of vegetarian options, breakfast and an excellent set lunch (1090Ft).

JÓZSEF ROSTA/LUDWIG MÚZEUM – MÚSEUM OF CONTEMPORARY ART ©

Ludwig Museum of Contemporary Art

Sights

Museum of Applied Arts MUSEUM

1 ◎ Map p114, C4

The Museum of Applied Arts has two permanent collections, one containing Hungarian furniture from the 18th and 19th centuries, Art Nouveau and Secessionist artefacts, and objects relating to trades and crafts (glass-making, bookbinding, goldsmithing), and the other Islamic Art from the 9th to the 19th centuries. It's housed in a gorgeous Ödön Lechner–designed building, decorated with Zsolnay ceramic tiles, and completed for the Millenary Exhibition in 1896.

(Iparművészeti Múzeum; www.imm.hu; IX Üllői út 33-37; adult/student 2000/1000Ft; ⊙10am-6pm Tue-Sun; Ⓜ M3 Corvin-negyed, 🚊4, 6)

Ludwig Museum of Contemporary Art MUSEUM

2 ◎ Map p114, B5

Housed in the architecturally controversial Palace of Arts opposite the National Theatre, the Ludwig Museum holds Hungary's most important collection of international contemporary art. Works by American, Russian, German and French artists span the past 50 years, while Hungarian, Czech, Slovakian, Romanian, Polish and Slovenian works date from the 1990s. The museum also holds frequent and very well received temporary exhibitions. The permanent collection closes at 6pm. (Ludwig Kortárs Művészeti Múzeum; www.ludwigmuseum.hu; IX Komor Marcell utca 1; adult/student & child 1300/650Ft; ⏲10am-6pm. temporary exhibitons to 8pm, Tue-Sun; 🚋2, 24, HÉV7 Közvágóhíd)

Holocaust Memorial Center
JEWISH

 Map p114, D4

The superb Holocaust Memorial Center opened in 2004 on the 60th anniversary of the start of the Holocaust in Hungary. The permanent exhibition traces the rise of anti-Semitism in Hungary and follows the path to genocide of Hungary's Jewish and Roma communities, from the deprivation of rights through the increasing removal of freedom and dignity and, finally, mass deportations to German death camps in 1944–45.
(Holokauszt Emlékközpont; www.hdke.hu; IX Páva utca 39; adult/child 1400/700Ft; ⏲10am-6pm Tue-Sun; Ⓜ M3 Corvin-negyed)

Eating

Múzeum
HUNGARIAN €€€

 Map p114, B2

This cafe-restaurant is the place to come if you like to dine in old-world style. It's still going strong after 130 years at the same location near the Hungarian National Museum. The goose-liver parfait (3400Ft) is to die for, the goose leg and cabbage

(3900Ft) iconic, and there's a good selection of Hungarian wines.
(📞1-267 0375; www.muzeumkavehaz.hu; VIII Múzeum körút 12; mains 3600-7200Ft; ⏲6pm-midnight Mon-Sat; Ⓜ M3/4 Kálvin tér)

Macska
VEGETARIAN €

 Map p114, D2

'Cat' is a peculiar little cafe-bar, with vegie and vegan dishes on the menu and felines in various guises as part of its decor. Chilled atmosphere, occasional DJ appearances and good beer. (www.facebook.com/macska23; VIII Bérkocsis utca 23; dishes 1000-2100Ft; ⏲6pm-1am Mon-Thu, 4pm-2am Fri & Sat; ✈; Ⓜ M4 Rákóczi tér, 🚋4, 6)

Építész Pince
HUNGARIAN €€

6 🍴 Map p114, B2

This basement restaurant behind the Hungarian National Museum is stunningly designed and why wouldn't it be? It's in the neoclassical headquarters of the Chamber of Hungarian Architects. The food is mostly Hungarian favourites; come for the decor, the artsy crowd and the gorgeous paved courtyard that's candlelit come dusk.
(📞1-266 4799; www.epiteszpince.hu; VIII Ötpacsirta utca 2; mains 1990-3790Ft; ⏲11am-10pm Mon-Thu, to midnight Fri & Sat; Ⓜ M3/4 Kálvin tér)

Rosenstein
HUNGARIAN, JEWISH €€€

7 🍴 Map p114, D1

A top-notch Hungarian restaurant in an unlikely location, with Jewish tastes and aromas and super service. Family run, it's been here for years, so expect everyone to know each other. The extensive menu features some interesting game dishes as well as daily lunch specials that are a steal at as little as 2200Ft.

(1-333 3492; www.rosenstein.hu; VIII Mosonyi utca 3; mains 2500-9950Ft; noon-11pm Mon-Sat; M M2/4 Keleti pályaudvar, 24)

Curry House INDIAN €€

8 Map p114, C2

This richly decorated and well-run Indian restaurant offers a warm welcome, attentive service, and a wide range of dishes. There are lots of options for vegetarians, as well as lunchtime thalis, succulent tandoori and accomplished curries.

(1-264 0297; www.curryhouse.hu; VIII Horánszky utca 1; mains 1800-3100Ft; 11am-11pm Tue-Sun; ; M M4 Rákóczi tér)

Drinking

Lumen CAFE

9 Map p114, C3

A relaxed gallery, cafe and bar with a little terrace on Mikszáth Kálmán tér, this joint roasts its own coffee and serves Hungarian and craft beer and wine. In the evenings it fills with an arty crowd who come for the eclectic program of live music and DJ nights.

(www.facebook.com/lumen.kavezo; VIII Mikszáth Kálmán tér 2-3; 8am-midnight Mon-Fri, from 10am Sat & Sun; ; M M3/4 Kálvin tér, 4, 6)

Élesztő RUIN PUB

10 Map p114, D4

This pub, set in a former glassblowing workshop, is appropriately named – *élesztő* means yeast – given its unrivalled selection of craft beer. With a brewery on site, 20 brews on draught and brewing courses, this is a hophead's dream.

(www.facebook.com/elesztohaz; IX Tűzoltó utca 22; 3pm-3am; M M3 Corvin-negyed, 4, 6)

Corvintető CLUB

11 Map p114, C1

On the top of the former Corvin department store, this excellent club, with stunning views from its open-air dance floor, holds a variety of nights from techno to rooftop cinema. If you can't face the stairs head next door (once you've paid) to bar Villa Negra and take a seat in the goods lift for a ride to the roof.

(www.corvinteto.com; VIII Blaha Lujza tér 1; cover 300-1200ft; 10pm-6am Wed-Sat; M M2 Blaha Lujza tér)

Shopping

Magyar Pálinka Háza DRINK

12 Map p114, B1

This large shop stocks hundreds of varieties of *pálinka* (fruit brandy). Szicsek is a premium choice.

(Hungarian Pálinka House; www.magyarpalinkahaza.hu; VIII Rákóczi út 17; 9am-7pm Mon-Sat; 7)

Top Sights
City Park

Getting There

Ⓜ The M1 from Vörösmarty tér to Hősök tere and Széchenyi fürdő.

🚌 No 70 from V Kossuth Lajos tér, 72 from V Arany János utca, 75 from XIII Jászai Mari tér.

City Park is Pest's green lung, an open space measuring almost a square kilometre that hosted most of the events during Hungary's 1000th anniversary celebrations in 1896. Most of the museums, galleries and important statues and monuments lie to the south of XIV Kós Károly. Activities and attractions of a less cerebral nature – the Capital Circus of Budapest, Budapest Zoo and the Széchenyi Baths – are to the north.

Heroes' Square & Millenary Monument

Don't Miss

Museum of Fine Arts

The **Museum of Fine Arts** (Szépművészeti Múzeum; www.mfab.hu; XIV Dózsa György út 41; adult/concession 1800/900Ft, temporary exhibitions 3200/1600Ft; ⊙10am-6pm Tue-Sun; MM1 Hősök tere) houses the city's most outstanding collection of foreign artworks in a building dating from 1906. The Old Masters collection, with thousands of works from the 13th to 18th centuries, includes seven paintings by El Greco. Other sections include Egyptian and classical artefacts, 19th- and 20th-century paintings, watercolours, graphics and sculpture.

Széchenyi Baths

At the northern end of City Park, the **Széchenyi Baths** (www.szechenyibath.hu; XIV Állatkerti körút 9-11; ticket incl locker/cabin Mon-Fri 4500/5000Ft, Sat & Sun 4700/5200Ft; ⊙6am-10pm) is unusual for three reasons: its immense size (with 15 indoor pools and three outdoor); its bright, clean atmosphere; and its water temperatures (up to 38°C), which really are what the wall plaques say they are. The thermal outdoor pools are open year-round.

Heroes' Square & Millenary Monument

Heroes' Sq is the largest and most symbolic square in Budapest, and contains the Millenary Monument, a 36m-high pillar backed by colonnades to the right and left. It was designed in 1896 to mark the 1000th anniversary of the Magyar conquest of the Carpathian Basin. At the top is the Archangel Gabriel and below a stone cenotaph called the Heroes Monument.

Budapest Zoo

The city's **zoo** (www.zoobudapest.com; XIV Állatkerti körút 6-12; adult/child/family 2500/1800/7300Ft; ⊙9am-6.30pm Mon-Thu, to 7pm Fri-Sun May-Aug, reduced hours

SYLVAIN SONNET/GETTY IMAGES ©

☑ Top Tips

▶ While away some time in a rowing boat (1800Ft per hour) on the park's lake.

▶ The **City Park Ice-Skating Rink** (Városligeti Műjégpálya; www.mujegpalya.hu; XIV Olof Palme sétány 5; ⊙9am-1pm & 4-8pm Mon-Fri, 10am-2pm & 4-8pm Sat & Sun mid-Nov–Feb; MM1 Hősök tere), Europe's largest outdoor skating area, operates on the lake's western edge.

▶ The neighbourhoods south and east of the park contain some of the capital's grandest Art Nouveau buildings.

✗ Take a Break

If it's Sunday head for **Gundel** (☎1-889 8100; www.gundel.hu; XIV Gundel Károly út 4; mains 3600-25,000Ft; ⊙noon-midnight; MM1 Hősök tere) and its famous brunch (11.30am to 3pm; 6800/3400Ft per adult/child). Otherwise book a lakeside table at **Robinson** (www.robinsonrestaurant.hu; XIV Városligeti tó; mains 3200-13,700Ft; ⊙11am-5pm & 6-11pm).

Understand
Chronicler Unknown

The odd statue of the hooded figure on the small island in the lake is that of **Anonymous**, the unknown chronicler at the court of King Béla III who wrote a history of the early Magyars. Note the pen with the shiny tip in his hand; writers (both real and aspirant) stroke it for inspiration.

Sep-Apr) has an excellent collection of big cats, hippopotamuses, polar bears and giraffes, and some of the themed houses are world class. Have a look at the Secessionist animal houses built in the early part of the 20th century, such as the Elephant House, with Zsolnay ceramics, and the Palm House, built by the Parisian Eiffel Company.

Palace of Art
Recalling a Greek temple, the **Palace of Art** (www.mucsarnok.hu; XIV Dózsa György út 37; adult/concession 1800/900Ft; ☺10am-6pm Tue, Wed & Fri-Sun, noon-8pm Thu) is among the city's largest exhibition spaces and focuses on contemporary visual arts, with three or four major exhibitions annually. Go for the venue itself and the excellent museum shop. Concerts are sometimes staged here as well.

Transportation Museum
The **Transportation Museum** (www.mmkm.hu; XIV Városligeti körút 11; adult/child 1600/800Ft; ☺10am-5pm Tue-Fri, to 6pm Sat & Sun May-Sep, reduced hours Oct-Apr) is a great place for kids. In old and new wings there are scale models of ancient trains (some of which run), classic late-19th-century cars, sailing boats and lots of those old wooden bicycles called 'bone-shakers'. There are a few hands-on exhibits. Outside there's a cafe in an old MÁV train coach.

Capital Circus of Budapest
Europe's only permanent big top, the **Capital Circus** (www.circus.hu; XIV Állatkerti körút 12/a; adult 1900-3900Ft, senior 1700-2900Ft, child 1500-2700Ft) has everything one would expect, including acrobats, big cats and daredevils on horseback. Performances are usually at 3pm Wednesday to Sunday, with additional shows at 11am and 7pm on Saturday and at 11am on Sunday, but call ahead or check the website.

Holnemvolt Park
Holnemvolt Park (www.zoobudapest.com/pannonpark; XIV Állatkerti körút 6-12; admission 500Ft, with zoo admission free), or 'Once Upon a Time' Park), an extension of the Budapest Zoo, offers a veritable menagerie that kids can pet, feed and ride. Added amusement is provided by a set of rather tame (but very child-friendly) rides including a carousel, a roller coaster and a fairy-tale boat.

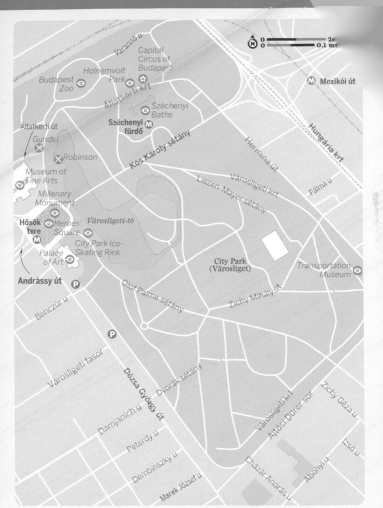

N 0 _____ 2€
0 _____ 0.1 mt

Varannó u

Capital Circus of Budapest

Holnemvolt Park

Budapest Zoo

Állatkerti krt

M Mexikói út

Széchenyi Baths

Széchenyi fürdő M

Állatkerti út

Gundel

Robinson

Kós Károly sétány

Hungária krt

Hermina út

Museum of Fine Arts

Millenary Monument

Városliget-tó

Liezen-Mayer sétány

Városligeti krt

Pálma u

Hősök tere M

Heroes' Square

City Park Ice-Skating Rink

City Park (Városliget)

Transportation Museum

Palace of Art

Andrássy út P

Olof Palme sétány

Zichy Mihály út

Benczúr u

P

Városligeti fasor

Dózsa György út

Dvořák sétány

Városligeti krt

Ajtósi Dürer sor

Zichy Géza u

Damjanich u

Peterdy u

Izsó u

Dembinszky u

Marek József u

Cházár András u

Abonyi u

The Best of
Budapest

Budapest's Best Walks

Budapest's Best...

Panorama of Budapest
ROMAN SIGAEV/SHUTTERSTOCK ©

Best Walks
Castle Hill

🏃 The Walk

There's no better introduction to Budapest than a tour of Castle Hill. The neighbourhood has everything that defines this delightful city: history, architecture, fabulous views and tourists in spades. If you'd like to take in the first three but avoid the last, make this an early-morning walk.

Start II Széll Kálmán tér

Finish II Clark Ádám tér

Length 1.2km; two hours

🍴 Take a Break

The Castle District is a picturesque and romantic neighbourhood in which to break bread, but if you want something a tad sweeter stop in at the hole-in-the wall **Budavári Rétesvár** (Strudel Castle; 📞06 70 314 2559; www.budavariretesvar.hu/; I Balta köz 4; strudel 299Ft, menu 990Ft; ⏰8am-7pm; 🚌16, 16A, 116), where strudel in all its permutations – from cherry and apple to dill with cheese and cabbage – is freshly baked daily.

Castle Hill (p22)

CULTURA TRAVEL/TIM E WHITE/GETTY IMAGES ©

❶ Vienna Gate

Walk up Várfok utca from Széll Kálmán tér to **Vienna Gate**, the medieval entrance to the Old Town and rebuilt in 1936 to mark the 250th anniversary of the retaking of the castle from the Turks. It's not that huge, but when loquacious Hungarian children natter on, their parents tell them: 'Be quiet, your mouth is as big as the Vienna Gate!'

❷ National Archives

The large building to the west with the superbly coloured majolica-tiled roof contains the National Archives (Országos Levéltár), completed in 1920. Note the attractive group of burgher houses across Bécsi kapu tér, site of a weekend market in the Middle Ages.

❸ Táncsics Mihály utca

Narrow Táncsics Mihály utca is full of little houses painted in lively hues and adorned with statues. In many courtyard entrances you'll see *sedilia*, medieval stone niches used as merchant stalls. The leader of the 1848–49 War of Independence,

Lajos Kossuth, was held in a prison at No 9 from 1837 to 1840.

④ Szentháromság tér

In the centre of **I Szentháromság tér** is a statue of the Holy Trinity, a 'plague pillar' first erected by grateful (and healthy) Buda citizens in the early 18th century. Across the square, the Hilton Budapest incorporates parts of a medieval Dominican church and a baroque Jesuit college.

⑤ Former Ministry of Defence

Walking along Úri utca south to Dísz tér you'll come across the restored **former Ministry of Defence**, a casualty of WWII, and NATO's supposed nuclear target for Budapest during the Cold War. A long-overdue renovation has just been completed.

⑥ Sándor Palace

Further south on the left is the restored **Sándor Palace** (Sándor palota), now housing the offices

of the president of the republic. A rather low-key guard change takes place in front of the palace hourly between 9am and 6pm.

⑦ Sikló

Between Sándor Palace and the the Habsburg Steps leading to the Royal Palace is the upper station of the **Sikló** (p25), the funicular that will take you down to I Clark Ádám tér just west of the Chain Bridge.

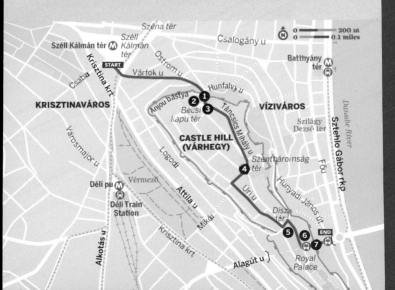

Best Walks
Erzsébetváros & the Jewish Quarter

🏃 The Walk

This section of Erzsébetváros, stretching between the Big and Little Ring Rds, has always been predominantly Jewish, and this was the ghetto where Jews were forced to live behind wooden fences when the Nazis occupied Hungary in 1944. Walking through its streets is like stepping back in time.

Start VI Liszt Ferenc tér

Finish VII Dohány utca

Length 1km; one to two hours

🍴 Take a Break

Even if you don't answer to a higher authority, why not try kosher food? **Carimama** (www.carimama.hu; VI Kazinczy utca 28; pizzas 2000-3000Ft; ⊘8am-8pm Sun-Thu, 7am-2hr before Shabat Fri; Ⓜ M2 Astoria), a little cafe opposite the Orthodox Synagogue, can oblige with kosher pizza, baked goods and breakfast, too.

Great Synagogue (p94)

❶ Liszt Academy

Begin the walk in restaurant- and cafe-packed VI Liszt Ferenc tér, where you should poke your head into the recently renovated **Liszt Academy** (p106) at the southeastern end.

❷ Church of St Teresa

Walking southwest along Király utca you'll pass the **Church of St Teresa**, built in 1811 and containing a massive neoclassical altar designed by Mihály Pollack a decade later.

❸ Klauzál tér

Turning into Csányi utca, head southeast over Dob utca to the heart of the Jewish Quarter, **Klauzál tér**. The square and surrounding streets retain a feeling of prewar Budapest. A continued Jewish presence is still evident – at the Carimama kosher bakery and pizzeria, the Fröhlich Cukrászda cake shop and cafe, and a butcher just next door to the Orthodox Synagogue.

❹ Ghetto Wall

Return to Dob utca, turn right onto Holló utca and then turn left. Enter the gate at Király utca 15 –

someone will obligingly buzz you in should it be locked – and at the rear of the courtyard is a 30m-long piece of the original **ghetto wall** rebuilt in 2010. Votive lamps and stones stand before it in tribute to victims of the Holocaust.

❺ Gozsdu udvar

The next turning on the left is a passageway called **Gozsdu udvar**, originally built in 1901, restored in 2009 and now emerging as the number-one nightlife destination in the district. It's lined with bars, cafes and restaurants and pulses with music and merrymaking come evening.

❻ Carl Lutz Monument

At Dob utca 12 is an unusual antifascist **monument to Carl Lutz,** a Swiss consul who, like Raoul Wallenberg, provided Jews with false papers in 1944. It portrays an angel on high sending down a long bolt of cloth to a victim.

❼ Rumbach Sebestyén Utca Synagogue

Just around the corner is the dilapidated

Moorish-style **Rumbach Sebestyén Utca Synagogue**, built in 1872 by Austrian Secessionist architect Otto Wagner for the Status Quo Ante (moderate conservative) community. The beautiful interior is slowly getting a long-awaited facelift.

❽ Great Synagogue

Retrace your steps and you'll see the twin towers of the Great Synagogue (p94) looming ahead of you at the end of the street.

Best
Eating

The dining scene in Budapest has undergone a sea change in recent years. Hungarian food has lightened up, offering the same wonderfully earthy and spicy tastes but in less calorific dishes. A number of vegetarian (or partly meatless) restaurants have opened, and the choice of eateries with cuisines other than Magyar is greater than ever before.

Hungarian Cuisine

You're likely familiar with some of the most common Hungarian dishes. *Gulyás* (goulash) is Hungary's signature dish, though here it's more like a soup than a stew and made with beef, onions and tomatoes. Paprika-infused *pörkölt* is closer to what we would call goulash. *Halászlé* is a highly recommended fish soup made from poached freshwater fish, tomatoes, green peppers and paprika. *Savanyúság* (literally 'sourness') is anything from mildly sour-sweet cucumbers to almost acidic sauerkraut eaten with a main course. A favourite dessert is *palincsinta*, a crêpe filled with jam, sweet cheese or chocolate sauce.

Types of Eateries

An *étterem* is a restaurant with a large selection, including international dishes. A *vendéglő* (or *kisvendéglő*) is smaller and usually serves inexpensive regional dishes or 'home cooking'. An *étkezde* or *kifőzde* is something like a diner, smaller and cheaper than *kisvendéglő* and often with counter seating. The overused term *csárda* originally signified a country inn with a rustic atmosphere, Gypsy music and hearty local dishes. Now any place that strings dried peppers on the wall and a couple of painted plates seems to call itself that. A *bisztró* is a much cheaper sit-down place that is often *önkiszolgáló* (self-service).

MICHELLE GRANT/GETTY IMAGES ©

☑ Top Tips

▶ Most restaurants are open from 10am or 11am to 11pm or midnight.

▶ Arrive by 9pm or 10pm (at the latest) to ensure being seated and served.

▶ It is advisable to book tables at midrange to top-end restaurants, especially at the weekend.

Best Haute Cuisine

Borkonyha The 'Wine Kitchen' is currently our favourite in Pest, Michelin accolades notwithstanding. (p81)

Csalogány 26 Haute cuisine *à la hongroise* in the heart of Buda. (p31)

Klassz Unusually for a wine restaurant, both the vintages and the food are top class. (p102)

Kisbuda Gyöngye *Fin-de-siècle* atmosphere in an antique-cluttered Óbuda eatery. (p55)

Múzeum Going strong into its second century, this place combines excellent service and top-notch cooking. (p116)

Best Local

Kádár Lunch-only *ét-kezde* on an atmospheric square. (p102)

Kisharang The *étkezde* of choice among Budapest cognoscenti. (p82)

Földes Józsi Konyhája Rustic little place with a good range of *főzelék* (vegetables in a roux) dishes. (p56)

Kéhli Vendéglő So famous that it appears in literature. (p55)

Kárpátia *A fin-de-siècle* stunner with Hungarian and Transylvanian speci-alities. (p69)

Best Asian & Subcontinental

Kis Parázs Excellent Thai with a loyal after-club following. (p102)

Curry House Warmly decorated and well-run Indian eatery. (p117)

Pándzsáb Tandoori Family-run hole-in-the-wall produces excellent Indian tandoori dishes. (p89)

Best Italian

Da Mario Our new fa-vourite Italian for superb pasta dishes and wood-fired pizzas. (p82)

Trattoria Toscana Pizza, pasta and antipasto with river views. (p70)

Best Fish & Seafood

Halkakas Fresh, simple and great-value fish dishes. (p70)

Horgásztanya Vendéglő Reliable Hungarian fish dishes by the Danube. (p32)

Új Sípos Halászkert The place to try one of many Hungarian fish soups. (p56)

bigfish Super-fresh fish and shellfish. (p103)

Best Jewish

Macesz Huszár Hungarian-Jewish clas-sics, done to perfection. (p103)

Spinoza Café An ... ble neighbourhood that serves old favou... and *klezmer* (Jewish fo... music). (p102)

Best Modern Hungarian

Laci Konyha Boutique and very eclectic eatery located in northern Pest. (p89)

Gepárd És Űrhajó In-spired Hungarian cuisine with fabulous river views. (p69)

Aranyszarvas Game dishes and more in the shadow of the castle. (p44)

Fióka Bistro and wine bar winning points for new-style Hungarian dishes. (p32)

Best for Good-Value Lunch

Vár Bistro Cheap and cheerful Hungarian fast food in the Castle Dis-trict. (p32)

Pick Ház Grab-and-go buffet good for sampling Hungary's iconic sau-sage. (p82)

Tranzit Art Café For-mer bus depot that's a reliable spot for cheap lunches. (p45)

Best
Drinking

NDOLF POMPE/GETTY IMAGES ©

In recent years Budapest has justifiably gained a reputation as one of Europe's top nightlife destinations. Alongside its age-old cafe culture, it offers a magical blend of unique drinking holes, fantastic wine, homegrown fire waters and emerging craft beers, all served up with a wonderful sense of fun.

Pubs & Bars

Drinking establishments in the city run the gamut from quirky pubs and bohemian bars to much more refined wine and cocktail bars. If you want to sample the local beer (most commonly Dreher, Kőbányai and Arany Ászok) head for a *söröző*, a 'pub' with *csapolt sör* (draught beer) served in a *pohár* (0.3L glass) or *korsó* (0.4L or 0.5L). A *borozó* or *bor pince* is a traditional establishment (usually a dive) serving wine. Modern wine bars serve wine by the deci (decilitre, 0.1L) so you can sample a wide range.

Cafes

The *kávéház* (cafe) has long been an integral part of Budapest's social life and old-style cafes, some of which date back as much as a century and a half, abound in Budapest. The new breed of coffee house roasts its own blends and imports specific beans.

Ruin Pubs & Garden Clubs

Unique to Budapest, *romkocsmák* (ruin pubs) began to appear in the city in the early 2000s when abandoned buildings were turned into pop-up bars. At the same time, during the city's long and very hot summers, so-called *kertek* (literally 'gardens' but here any outdoor entertainment zone) empty out even the most popular indoor bars and clubs.

☑ Top Tips

Pest's two main nightlife strips are trendy VI Liszt Ferenc tér, where you'll have to fight for a spot under the plane trees, and IX Ráday utca, a more subdued pedestrianised street in Józsefváros full of pubs, bars and modern cafes. Up and coming is V Szent István tér behind the basilica.

Best Bars & Pubs

Szatyor Bár és Galéria Funky bar with street art and Hadik Kávéház as an annexe. (p46)

Tip Top Bar Tip-top views from alfresco rooftop bar. (p70)

Kisüzem Relaxed back-street find in the heart

of the nightlife district. (p97)

Telep Gallery and exhibition space moonlighting as a watering hole. (p97)

Akvárium Klub A variety of live music where buses once roamed. (p71)

Best Wine & Cocktail Bars

DiVino Borbár The place to taste your way though Hungary's wine regions. (p82)

Doblo Romantic brick-lined bar with a huge variety of Hungarian wine. (p104)

Oscar American Bar Film decor and cool cocktails below the castle. (p61)

Kadarka Sociable wine bar with a huge list. (p97)

Best Clubs

A38 Watertight watering hole voted the world's best. (p46)

Corvinteto Rooftop dance floor with quality DJs and a view right across the city. (p117)

GMK Cool cavern with an excellent sound system. (p97)

Anker Klub Very central cafe that becomes a hipster hangout. (p105)

Best Ruin Bars & Garden Clubs

Holdudvar Something for everyone at this most outdoor of garden clubs. (p90)

Instant Multilevel venue with a bar for every taste. (p82)

Mika Tivadar Mulató Fairy-lit garden with boats to take you a-cruising. (p97)

Lokál Ruin pub with swing dancing, fancy-

dressing, escape and tattooing. (p10

Élesztő High-quality craft beer, and lots of r (p117)

Best Traditional Cafes

Ruszwurm Cukrászda Dating back to the early 19th century, this is the oldest traditional cafe in town. (p33)

Szalai Cukrászda Forget the decor – go for the memorable cherry strudel. (p83)

Művész Kávéház People-watch with the Hungarian State Opera House as backdrop. (p104)

Gerbeaud Dating back to 1858 and still serving impeccable cakes and coffee. (p65)

Alexandra Book Cafe Glamour, glitz and Károly Lotz frescoes at the back of a bookshop. (p104)

Best
Shopping

THEPURPLEDOOR/GETTY IMAGES ©

Budapest is a fantastic city for shopping, whether you're in the market for traditional folk craft with a twist, cutting-edge designer goods, the latest in flash headgear or honey-sweet dessert wine. Traditional markets stand side by side with mammoth shopping malls, and old-style umbrella makers can still be found next to avant-garde fashion boutiques.

Specialities & Souvenirs

Traditional items with a Hungarian branding – called Hungarica here – include folk embroidery and ceramics, pottery, wall hangings, painted wooden toys and boxes, dolls, all types of basketry, and porcelain (especially that from Herend and Zsolnay). Feather or goose-down pillows and duvets (comforters) are of exceptionally high quality.

Foodstuffs that are expensive or difficult to buy elsewhere – goose liver (both fresh and potted), dried mushrooms, jam (especially the apricot variety), prepared meats like Pick salami, the many types of paprika – make nice gifts (as long as you're allowed to take them into your country). Some of Hungary's boutique wines also make excellent gifts.

Markets

Some people consider a visit to one of Budapest's flea markets not just an opportunity to indulge their consumer vices but the consummate Budapest experience. Make sure you visit one of the city's 20 large food markets, most of them in Pest. The majority are closed on Sunday, and Monday is always very quiet.

☑ **Top Tips**

Some streets specialise in certain goods or products.

▶ **Antiques** V Falk Miksa utca (Pest) and II Frankel Leó út (Buda).

▶ **Antiquarian and secondhand books** V Múzeum körút (Pest).

▶ **Boutiques and souvenirs** V Váci utca (Pest).

▶ **International fashion brands** V Deák Ferenc utca (Pest).

▶ **Local designer goods and fashion** VI Király utca (Pest).

Best Gifts & Souvenirs

XD Design & Souvenir Excellent choice for 'Made in Hungary' traditional gifts as well as some cracking newly designed items. (p71)

Herend Village Pottery Big, bold and colourful platters make a lovely change from traditional Herend porcelain. (p34)

Bomo Art The finest paper and paper goods are sold here. (p71)

Best for Food & Drink

Bortársaság The first port of call for buying wine. (p34)

Magyar Pálinka Háza Shelves and shelves of all kinds of *pálinka* (fruit brandy). (p117)

Mézes Kuckó Still the best place for nut-and-honey cookies. (p91)

Rózsavölgyi Csokoládé Artisan chocolate bars and bonbons, beautifully packaged. (p71)

Best for Fashion & Clothing

Valeria Fazekas Beautiful designer millinery. (p71)

Printa Locally designed bags, leather goods and T-shirts. (p106)

Vass Shoes Classic footwear – cobbled for you or ready to wear. (p65)

Balogh Kesztyű Üzlet Bespoke handwear that will fit like a proverbial glove. (p65)

Best for Books

Bestsellers Budapest's most complete English-language bookshop; helpful staff. (p83)

Massolit New and secondhand in an atmospheric old shop with a little garden. (p106)

Múzeum Antikvárium Used and antique books opposite the Hungarian National Museum. (p113)

Best for Antiques

BÁV Check out any branch of this pawn and secondhand shop chain if you can't make it to the flea markets. (p83)

Pintér Antik Budapest's largest retail antique shop. (p83)

Best Markets

Nagycsarnok Huge market hall selling everything from fruit and veg to paprika and goose liver. (p112)

Rákóczi tér market Authentic local market with products fresh from the farm. (p113)

Gouba Weekly arts and crafts market in the heart of Erzsébetváros. (p106)

Worth a Trip

One of the biggest flea markets in Central Europe, **Ecseri Piac** (www.piaconline.hu; XIX Nagykőrösi út 156; 8am-4pm Mon-Fri, 5am-3pm Sat, 8am-1pm Sun) sells everything from antique jewellery and Soviet army watches to top hats. Saturday is the best day to go. Take bus 54 from Boráros tér in Pest or express bus 84E, 89E or 94E from the Határ út stop on the M3 metro line.

Best
With Kids

Budapest abounds in places that will delight children, and there is always a special child (and often a family) entry rate to paying attractions. Visits to many areas of the city can be designed around a rest stop or picnic – at City Park, say, or on Margaret Island.

ROBERTO SONCIN GEROMETTA/GETTY IMAGES ©

Best Museums & Galleries

Transportation Museum Great for kids, with lots of show-and-tell explanations from enthusiastic attendants. (p120)

Museum of Fine Arts Program allows kids to handle original Egyptian artefacts and create their own works of art. (p119)

Aquincum Museum Great interactive exhibits, including virtual duelling with a gladiator. (p59)

Best Entertainment

Capital Circus of Budapest Europe's only permanent big top delights children of all ages. (p120)

Budapest Puppet Theatre Kids will be transfixed by the marionette shows even if they don't speak Hungarian. (p106)

Budapest Zoo World-class collection of big cats, hippopotamuses, polar bears and giraffes. (p119)

Holnemvolt Park Fun amusement rides at the northern end of City Park. (p120)

Best Children's Táncház

Aranytíz Cultural Centre Regularly scheduled kids' *táncház* on Saturday afternoon. (p83)

Municipal Cultural House The folk group Muzsikás runs a *táncház* for children on Tuesday evening. (p46)

Best Public Transport

Sikló Climbing up to Castle Hill at an angle. (p25)

☑ **Top Tips**

Budapest's traditional cafes and *cukrászdák* (cake shops) will satisfy a sweet tooth of any size, but for a really special occasion treat the little rascals to the all-you-can-eat dessert bar at the Budapest Marriott Hotel. Just 2200Ft gets you as many cakes as they can manage from noon to 10pm daily.

Cog Railway This unusual conveyance will delight kids. (p61)

Children's Railway Kids in charge in the Buda Hills. (p61)

Best
Thermal Baths & Pools

Budapest lies on a geological fault, and mineral water gushes forth daily from more than 120 thermal springs. As a result, the city is a major spa centre and 'taking the waters' at one of the city's many baths, be they Turkish time warps, Art Nouveau marvels or modern establishments, is a real Budapest experience.

What's Inside

The layout of most of Budapest's baths follows a similar pattern: a series of indoor thermal pools, where temperatures range from warm to hot, with steam rooms, saunas, ice-cold plunge pools and rooms for massage. Some have swimming pools.

Getting In & Out

All baths and pools have cabins or lockers. You are usually given an electronic bracelet that directs you to, and then opens, your locker or cabin. Ask for assistance if you can't work it out. Others employ the old, more personal method Find an empty locker or

cabin yourself, and after getting changed in (or beside) it, seek out an attendant, who will lock it for you and hand you a numbered tag to tie onto your swimming costume.

Rudas Baths Built in 1566, these are the most Turkish of all in Budapest. (p44)

Gellért Baths Soaking in these Art Nouveau baths is like bathing in a cathedral. (p40)

Veli Bej Baths A venerable Turkish bath in Buda resurrected after centuries. (p54)

Széchenyi Baths With 15 thermal baths and three outdoor swimming pools in City Park. (p119)

☑ Top Tips

▶ Fewer and fewer baths have male- and female-only days, so pack a bathing suit or rent one (1000Ft).

▶ Some pools require bathing caps. Buy a disposable one for 200Ft.

▶ You might consider taking along a pair of plastic sandals or flip-flops. Floors can be slippery.

Király Baths The four small Turkish pools here date to 1565. (p30)

Danubius Health Spa Margitsziget Modern spa with up-to-date facilities and an enviable choice of special treatments. (p88)

Best **Entertainment**

For a city its size, Budapest has a huge choice of things to do and places to go after dark – from opera and folk dancing to live jazz and films screened in palatial cinemas. It's usually not difficult getting tickets or getting in; the hard part is deciding what to do and where to go.

RENAUD VISAGE/GETTY IMAGES ©

Best for Classical Music & Dance

Liszt Academy Budapest's premier venue for classical concerts is also an Art Nouveau treasure house. (p106)

Palace of Arts The city's most up-to-date cultural venue with two concert halls and near-perfect acoustics. (p120)

Hungarian State Opera House Small but perfectly formed home to both the state opera company and the Hungarian National Ballet. (p100)

Budapest Operetta Campy fun for the whole family in the theatre district. (p83)

Best for Táncház

Municipal Cultural House Your chance to hear the incomparable group Muzsikás. (p46)

Aranytíz Cultural Centre Hosts the wonderful Kalamajka Táncház on Saturday. (p83)

Marczibányi tér Cultural Centre Not just Magyar but Slovakian and Moldavian dance and music too. (p34)

Best for Jazz & Blues

Budapest Jazz Club Reliable music venue still swings in its new location. (p91)

Jedermann Relaxed Ráday utca hangout for jazz and great grills. (p113)

Best for Live Music

Spinoza Café An excellent place to hear *klezmer* (Jewish folk) music. (p102)

Akvárium Klub In an old bus terminal, two large

Top Tips

▶ Useful freebies for popular listings include **Budapest Funzine** (www.budapestfunzine.hu) and **PestiEst** (www.est.hu) and, for more serious offerings, the **Koncert Kalendárium** (www.muzsikalendarium.hu/) website.

▶ You can book online from the following sites, including **Jegymester** (www.jegymester.hu) and **Ticket Express.** (www.tex.hu)

halls serve up a quality line-up of live acts. (p71)

Gödör Great gigs in the midst of banging Erzsébetváros. (p106)

Best
Architecture

Budapest's architectural waltz through history begins with the Romans at Aquincum, moves up to Castle Hill's medieval streets, over to the ruins of Margaret Island and into the many splendid baroque churches on either side of the Danube. Neoclassicism chips in with the Basilica of St Stephen and the Hungarian National Museum. But the capital really hits its stride with its Art Nouveau masterpieces.

PETR SVARC/GETTY IMAGES ©

Roman

Aquincum A 2nd-century paved street and outlines of houses and public buildings in Óbuda. (p59)

Contra Aquincum Remains of a Roman fort in the heart of the Inner Town. (p71)

Medieval

Inner Town Parish Church Side chapels with some fine Gothic and Renaissance tabernacles. (p68)

Castle Museum Highlights include the Gothic Hall, Royal Cellar and 14th-century Tower Chapel. (p27)

Margaret Island Remains of an early Franciscan church and

monastery and a Dominican convent. (p84)

Turkish Era

Rudas Baths Octagonal pool, domed cupola and massive columns from the 16th century. (p44)

Gül Baba's Tomb Mosque and last resting place of a 16th-century dervish. (p54)

Király Baths Another great structure dating from Turkish times with a wonderful skylit central dome. (p30)

Baroque

Holy Trinity Statue Stunning example of ecclesiastical baroque on Castle Hill.

Citadella The best example of civic (or secular) baroque in Budapest. (p38)

Neoclassical

Hungarian National Museum Textbook example of this style from the late 1840s. (p110)

Basilica of St Stephen The dome is the giveway of this neoclassical delight that took 50 years to build. (p76)

Art Nouveau

Museum of Applied Arts Zsolnay roof tiles, central marble hall and 'Moghul' turrets and domes. (p115)

Philanthia Probably the most complete Art Nouveau interior in Budapest. (p65)

Best
Gay & Lesbian

Budapest offers just a reasonable gay scene for its size. Most gay people are discreet in public places. Lesbian social life remains very much underground, with a lot of private parties. There have been a couple of violent right-wing demonstrations in response to Budapest Pride celebrations in the recent past. Attitudes are changing, but society generally remains conservative on this issue.

NP/SHUTTERSTOCK ©

Best Gay Venues

Club AlterEgo Still the city's premier gay club (and don't you forget it) with the best dance music. (p82)

Score Club The (only) place to do just that in Buda attracts a slightly older crowd. (p34)

Action Bar Basement bar with a weekly strip show – for those seriously out for business. (p70)

CoXx Men's Bar Three bars and a whole new world of subterranean cruising. (p105)

Best Gay-Friendly Accommodation

KM Saga Guest Residence Quirky residence with over-the-top decor still manages to feel like home. (p145)

Casati Tasteful conversion in the centre of Pest with cool decor and funky covered courtyard. (p145)

☑ **Top Tips**

Useful gay and lesbian resources include the following:

▶ **Gay Budapest** (www.budapest-gay.com) Of some use for accommodation.

▶ **Háttér Society** (www.hatter.hu) Advice and help line.

▶ **Labrisz** (www.labrisz.hu) Lesbian Association Info on the city's lesbian scene.

▶ **Radio Pink** (http://radiopink.hu) Budapest's gay radio station, broadcast through web-based live stream.

Best
Tours

ART BLACK/GETTY IMAGES ©

Bus Tours

Program Centrum Valid on two bus routes (one taped in 24 languages, one live commentary in English and German) and a one-hour river cruise for 48 hours. (www.programcentrum.hu)

Cityrama If you prefer to stay on the bus, this operator offers three-hour city tours, with several photo stops and live commentary in five languages. (www.cityrama.hu)

Boat Tours

Mahart PassNave One-hour trip between Margaret and Rákóczi bridges departs hourly. (www.mahartpassnave.hu)

Legenda Similar deal in 30 languages has between five and six daily departures but only in winter. (www.legenda.hu)

River Ride Amphibious bus takes you on a two-hour heart-stopping tour of Budapest by road and river; live commentary (English and German). (www.riverride.com)

Cycle Tours

Yellow Zebra Bikes Tours take in Heroes' Sq, City Park, central Pest and Castle Hill in around four hours and include the bike. Depart from in front of the Discover Budapest office behind the Opera House at 11am daily from April to October (also at 5pm July and August). In winter departures are at 11am on Friday, Saturday and Sunday only. (www.yellowzebrabikes.com)

Walking Tours

Free Budapest Tours A 2½-hour tour of both Pest and Buda leaves from V Deák Ferenc tér (opposite Le Meridien Hotel) daily at 10.30am, and the 1½-hour tour of Pest leaves from the same place at 2.30pm. Guides work for tips only, so dig deep into your pockets. (www.freebudapesttours.eu)

☑ **Top Tips**

The **Budapest Card** includes two free guided tours and offers discounts on other organised tours. (p148)

Paul Street Tours Personal walking tours covering the Castle District (about two hours), less-explored areas of Pest, such as the Jewish Quarter and Andrássy út (two to three hours), the Little Ring Rd, the parks and gardens of Budapest, and shopping, with lots of anecdotal information on architecture and social history. Available by appointment year-round. (www.paulstreettours.com)

Best
Parks & Gardens

Budapest and vicinity counts some eight protected landscape areas and more than 30 nature conservation areas. The largest area within the city proper encompasses the Buda Hills, the lungs of the city and a 10,500-hectare protected area of steep ravines, rocky grasslands and more than 150 caves. Less 'wild' green spaces can be found through the city on both sides of the Danube.

GEORGE TSAFOS/GETTY IMAGES ©

City Park Enormous City Park is filled with (mostly paid) attractions, but entry to the park is free. (p118)

Margaret Island The island is replete with gardens, most notably the Japanese Garden at the northern end. (p84)

Gellért Hill On the south side of Gellért Hill, Jubilee Park has trails and is an ideal spot for a picnic. (p36)

Buda Hills A magnet for hikers, the hills also con-

tain a number of nature reserves. (p60)

Budapest Zoo Not just a menagerie but a botanical garden too, with a Japanese Garden and Palm House. (p119)

Károly Garden The oldest public garden in the city is hidden deep in the Inner Town. (p70)

Szabadság tér The gardens in this huge square are often overlooked in favour of the grandiose buildings around it. (p80)

☑ **Top Tips**

The best time to take a walk in Budapest's parks is in mid- or late spring when the flowers and trees are in full blossom. These green places also provide shade from the scorching summer heat. A walk in a park between mid-September and mid-October will reward with beautiful foliage, though winter is often rather bleak.

Best
Museums & Galleries

Unlike most other European cities, Budapest does not have a single museum founded from a royal treasury. Instead, support came from an increasingly politicised aristocracy, which saw the value of safeguarding the nation's relics and artwork. Today the city counts some five dozen museums devoted to subjects as diverse as op art, musical instruments, trade and tourism and folk costume.

History Museums

Aquincum Museum Purpose-built museum with large collection of Roman finds. (p59)

Castle Museum Renovated museum walks you through Budapest history painlessly. (p27)

Art Museums

Vasarely Museum Devoted to op art – and still as whacky and mesmerising as ever. (p54)

Hungarian National Gallery Treasure house of the most important Hungarian artwork. (p25)

Museum of Applied Arts Come for the sumptuous interior and vast collection of Art Nouveau furniture. (p115)

Ludwig Museum of Contemporary Art Budapest's foremost assembly of European and Hungarian modern art. (p115)

Cultural Museums

Memento Park Last resting place of Communist-era statues and monuments. (p49)

Music History Museum Filled with scores and musical instruments that play. (p31)

Hungarian Museum of Trade & Tourism The catering and hospitality trade through objects and advertising. (p54)

Hungarian Jewish Museum The story of Hungarian Jewry from the time of the Romans until the Holocaust. (p95)

GEORGE TSAFOS/GETTY IMAGES ©

☑ Top Tips

▶ Wear comfortable shoes and make use of the cloakrooms.

▶ Standing still and walking slowly promote tiredness; whenever possible, sit down.

▶ Reflecting on the material and forming associations with it causes information to move from your short- to long-term memory; your experiences will thus amount to more than a series of visual 'bites'.

▶ Choose a particular period or section and pretend that the rest of the museum is somewhere across town.

Best
Escape Games

In the last few years, Budapest has seen the emergence of a new, quirky and justifiably popular activity: live escape games, in which teams of between two and six people willingly lock themselves into a set of rooms in order to spend 60 minutes working through numerous riddles that will eventually unlock the door back to freedom.

EPA EUROPEAN PRESSPHOTO AGENCY B.V. / ALAMY ©

Distinct Themes & Stories

Similar to the city's ruin pubs, the games are often set in empty and disused apartment blocks, especially their dank and atmospheric basements. Each game has a distinct theme and story – from Ancient Egypt and medieval to Cold War and sci-fi – and involves not only the solving of puzzles but, crucially, the ability to identify the puzzles in the first place. Mentally challenging, the games are incredibly addictive and popular with tourists and locals alike; it's estimated that Budapest now has as many as 100 of them. No Hungarian

is required and it's best to book in advance, although you may get lucky if you just show up.

Parapark The city's first escape game, now with three themes, set in the basement of a ruin pub. (www.parapark.hu)

TRAP 'Team Race Against Puzzles'; great for solo travellers, who can use the find-a-team-mate function on the website. (www.trap.hu)

Claustrophilia Skillfully choreographed escape game that begins the moment you enter; has two locations. (www.claustrophilia.hu)

MindQuest Three escape rooms: a bomb to defuse, a diamond to

steal and a matrix to outwit. (www.mindquest.hu)

☑ Top Tips

▶ Don't waste time; try all of your ideas.

▶ Search everywhere – look up, under and behind, and go back and forth between spaces.

▶ Share your findings with your team.

▶ Don't be ashamed to ask for help – your captors will happily give you clues.

▶ Don't think too hard – make sure you enjoy it!

Survival Guide

Survival Guide

Before You Go

When to Go

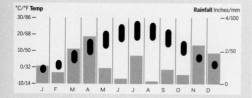

➡ **Spring (Apr–Jun)** Often wet, but just glorious, with fewer tourists.

➡ **Summer (Jul & Aug)** Warm, sunny and unusually long, with a lot of festivals, but expect higher prices and long queues.

➡ **Autumn (Sep & Oct)** Beautiful, particularly in the Buda Hills, and festivals mark the *szüret* (grape harvest); holiday-makers have gone home.

➡ **Winter (Nov–Mar)** Can be cold and bleak; some attractions curtail their hours.

Book Your Stay

➡ In general, accommodation in the Buda neighbourhoods is more limited than on the other side of the Danube River in Pest.

➡ A cheap hotel is generally more expensive than a private room but may be the answer if you are only staying one night or arrive too late to get a room through an agency.

➡ Travel agencies levy a surcharge (at least for the first night) if you stay fewer than three nights in a private room.

➡ Budapest levies a 4% local tourist tax on visitors over 18.

➡ The quoted rates usually include breakfast, but check.

☑ **Top Tip** Some top-end hotels in Budapest do not include the whopping 18% VAT on accommodation in their listed rack rates; make sure you read the bottom line.

Useful Websites

Lonely Planet (www.lonelyplanet.com/budapest) Find reviews and book online.

Booking.com (www.booking.com) Tried and tested.

Budapest Info (http://old.budapestinfo.hu) Book through the tourist office.

Xpatloop Classifieds (www.xpatloop.com/classifieds) Contains adverts for longer rentals.

Caboodle (www.caboodle.hu) Useful and thorough lists of three-, four- and five-star hotels.

Best Budget

Maverick City Lodge (www.maverick-lodges.com) Modern, warehouse-style hostel with great facilities.

Shantee House (www.backpackbudapest.hu) Budapest's first hostel grows (up) in size and design.

Aventura Boutique Hostel (www.aventurahostel.com) Colourful number that shuns bunk beds and curfews.

Hotel Császár (www.csaszarhotel.hu) Small

but perfectly formed, with an Olympic-size pool attached.

KM Saga Guest Residence (www.km-saga.hu) Wonderfully eccentric and good-value rooms full of 19th-century furnishings.

Best Midrange

Gerlóczy Rooms deLux (www.gerloczy.hu) Tastefully designed, homey accommodation in a quiet central square.

Baltazár (http://baltazarbudapest.com/) Hotel with a high-end Castle location.

Casati (www.casatibudapesthotel.com) An artful conversion of a beautiful building with sustainable credentials.

Budapest Rooms (www.budapestrooms.eu) Well run, good-looking B&B with a very helpful host.

Hotel Papillon (www.hotelpapillon.hu) Delightful country-style hotel in the Buda Hills.

Best Top End

Four Seasons Gresham Palace Hotel (www.fourseasons.com/budapest) Still the city's most luxurious hotel, risen phoenix-

like from a derelict Art Nouveau palace.

Hotel Palazzo Zichy (www.hotel-palazzo-zichy.hu) Period features and ultra-modern design seamlessly combine in this sumptuous palace.

Danubius Hotel Gellért (www.danubiusgroup.com/gellert) A historic hotel with a historic spa.

Lánchíd 19 (www.lanchid19hotel.hu) Award-winning boutique hotel with stunning design both inside and out.

Zara Boutique Hotel (www.boutiquehotelbudapest.com) Charming boutique style in the Belváros, steps from the Danube.

Best Short-Stay Apartments

Katona Apartments (www.kartik.hu) Simply furnished and cleverly arranged apartments in a quiet old block.

Residence Izabella (www.residence-izabella.com) Fabulous conversion of a 19th-century Eclectic building just off swanky Andrássy út.

Arriving in Budapest

☑ **Top Tip** For the best way to get to the area where your accommodation is located, see p17.

Ferenc Liszt International Airport

➡ Budapest has two modern terminals side by side 24km southeast of the city centre. Most international flights land at Terminal 2A.

➡ Fő Taxi has the monopoly on picking up taxi passengers at the airport; to Pest it's about 6000Ft, to Buda around 7000Ft. You can take any taxi *to* the airport.

➡ Airport Shuttle Minibusz ferries passengers to/from the airport in nine-seat vans directly to/from their hotel, hostel or residence. Be warned: you may have to wait while the van fills up.

➡ A cheap but slow option: take bus 200E (350Ft, on the bus 450Ft; 4am to midnight) to the Kőbánya-Kispest metro station and then the

M3 metro into the city centre. Total cost: 700Ft to 800Ft.

Keleti, Nyugati & Déli Train Stations

➡ All three train stations are on metro lines of the same name.

➡ Keleti is on both the green M4 and the blue M3 lines. Nyugati is on the M3. Déli is on the red M2 line.

➡ Night buses serve all three stations when the metro is closed.

Stadion & Népliget Bus Stations

➡ Both international bus stations are on metro lines.

➡ Népliget is on the blue metro M3 (station: Népliget). Stadion is on the red metro M2 (station: Stadionok).

International Ferry Pier

➡ The International Ferry Pier, where the hydrofoils to and from Vienna dock, is on the tram 2 line, and is close to the Fővám tér station of the M4 metro line.

Getting Around

Metro

☑ **Best for...**speedy travel throughout the day, especially at rush hour.

➡ Budapest has four underground metro lines. Three of them (M1, M2 and M3) converge at Deák Ferenc tér (only). The new M4 links with the M2 at Keleti pályaudvar and with the M3 at Kálvin tér.

➡ Runs daily from 4am to about 11.15pm.

➡ The basic fare for the metro and all other forms of transport is 350Ft (3000Ft for a block of 10).

➡ Tickets must be validated at metro entrances.

Bus

☑ **Best for...**reliable transport around the clock.

➡ Extensive network of regular buses on 260 routes from around 4.15am to between 9pm and 11.30pm.

➡ From 11.30pm to just after 4am a network of 40 night buses (three digits beginning with '9')

operates every 15 to 60 minutes, depending on the route.

Tram

☑ **Best for...**sightseeing along the way.

➡ Trams run on 30 lines and are faster and more frequent than buses.

➡ The most useful trams follow the ring roads, including tram 6, which runs every 10 to 15 minutes round the clock.

Taxi

☑ **Best for...**quick trips around town and easy night-time travel.

➡ Taxis are cheap by European standards, with uniform flag fall (450Ft) and per-kilometre charges (280Ft).

➡ Never get into a taxi that does not have a yellow license plate and an identification badge displayed on the dashboard (as required by law), the logo of one of the reputable taxi firms on the outside of the side doors and a table of fares clearly visible on the right-side back door.

➡ Reputable operators include City Taxi, Fő Taxi, Rádió Taxi and Taxi 4.

Tickets & Passes

The basic fare for all forms of transport is 350Ft (3000Ft for a block of 10), allowing you to travel as far as you like on the same metro, bus or tram line without changing/transferring. A 'transfer ticket' allowing unlimited stations with one change within one hour costs 530Ft. Tickets bought on the bus and all night buses cost 450Ft.

A 24-hour travel card is poor value at 1650Ft, but the 72-hour one for 4150Ft and the seven-day pass for 4950Ft are worthwhile for most people. You'll need a photo for the fortnightly/monthly passes (7000/10,500Ft). The most central place to buy them is the ticket office at the Deák Ferenc tér metro station open from 6am to 11pm daily.

Essential Information

☑ **Top Tip** Opening hours (*nyitvatartás*) of any concern are always posted on the front door. *Nyitva* means open; *zárva* closed.

Business Hours

Standard business hours are as follows, unless specified in the review:

Banks 7.45am to 5pm or 6pm Monday, to 4pm or 5pm Tuesday to Thursday, to 4pm Friday.

Bars 11am to midnight Sunday to Thursday, to between 2am and 4am Friday and Saturday.

Businesses 9am or 10am to 6pm Monday to Friday, to 1pm Saturday.

Clubs 4pm to 2am Sunday to Thursday, to 4am Friday and Saturday; some open only weekends.

Grocery stores and supermarkets 6am or 7am to 7pm Monday to Friday, 7.30am to 3pm Saturday; some 7am to noon Sunday.

Restaurants 10am or 11am to 11pm or midnight.

Shops 9am or 10am to 6pm Monday to Friday, to 1pm Saturday, some to 8pm Thursday.

...ount Cards

...dapest Card (📞1-438
...80; www.budapestinfo.
...u; per 24/48/72hr
4500/7500/8900Ft) This
card gives you free
admission to selected
museums and other
sights in and around the
city; unlimited travel on all
forms of public transport;
two free guided tours; and
discounts for organised
tours, car rental, thermal
baths and selected shops
and restaurants. Available
at tourist offices but
cheaper online.

Electricity

220V/50Hz

Emergency

Any crime must be
reported at the police station of the district you are
in; if possible, bring along
a Hungarian speaker to
help.

Ambulance (📞1- 311 1666
(in English), 104)

**Belváros-Lipótváros
Police Station** (📞1-373
1000; V Szalay utca 11; Ⓜ M2
Kossuth Lajos tér)

General Emergency
(📞112)

Fire (📞105)

Police (📞107)

Internet Access

➡ Almost without
exception wireless (wi-fi)
access is available at hostels and hotels, though a
few of the latter charge a
fee for the service. Many
restaurants, cafes and
bars offer wi-fi, usually
free to paying customers.

➡ Most hostels and some
hotels have at least one
computer terminal avail-
able to guests either free
or for a nominal sum.

Media

Budapest has two
English-language news-
papers: **Budapest Times**
(www.budapesttimes.hu;

750Ft), a thin weekly with
straightforward news,
opinion pieces and some
reviews appearing on
Friday, and the fortnightly
**Budapest Business Jour-
nal** (www.bbj.hu; 1250Ft), an
almost archival publica-
tion of financial news
and business, appearing
every other Friday.

Money

☑ **Top Tip** It's always
prudent to carry a little
foreign cash in euros or
US dollars in case you
can't find an ATM nearby.

➡ **Currency** Hungary's
currency is the forint
(Ft). Prices in shops and
restaurants are in forint,
but many hotels and
guesthouses state their
prices in euros.

➡ **ATMs** Everywhere in
Budapest, including in
train and bus stations
and at airport terminals.

➡ **Credit Cards** Widely
accepted at restaurants,
shops, hotels and travel
agencies.

➡ **Moneychangers** Avoid
(especially the ones on
Váci utca) in favour of
banks.

➡ **Tipping** Widely
practised. In restaurants
never leave the money
on the table but tell the

Money-Saving Tips

➡ Some museums offer free entry on a certain day of the month.

➡ Buy a travel card, which will save both money and time.

➡ Consider buying the Budapest Card online.

➡ Set lunches at fine restaurants cost a fraction of set menus at dinner; eat by day and snack by night.

waiter how much to take out (usually around 10%).

Public Holidays

☑ **Top Tip** Transport out of Budapest can filll up on major holidays.

Hungary celebrates 10 *ünnep* (holidays) each year.

New Year's Day 1 January

National Day 15 March

Easter Monday March/April

Labour Day 1 May

Whit Monday May/June

St Stephen's Day 20 August

1956 Remembrance Day/Republic Day 23 October

All Saints' Day 1 November

Christmas holidays 25 and 26 December

Safe Travel

➡ Men should beware of being chatted up by so-called *konzumlányok*, attractive 'consume girls' in collusion with rip-off bars and clubs who will see you relieved of a serious chunk of money.

➡ Taxi drivers have been known to take advantage of passengers unfamiliar with local currency by switching large-denomination notes for smaller ones and demanding extra payment. Only ever take taxis from reputable companies and make sure you know exactly how much cash you're handing over.

➡ Waiters may try to bring you an unordered dish, make a 'mistake' when tallying the bill, or add service to the bill and then expect an additional tip. If you think there's a discrepancy, ask for the menu and check the bill carefully.

☑ **Top Tip** Do not even think of riding 'black' (without paying a fare) on public transport – you will be caught and fined.

Telephone

☑ **Top Tip** All localities in Hungary have a two-digit area code, except for Budapest, which has just a '1'.

➡ Phonecards come in values of 1000Ft, 2000Ft and 5000Ft and are available from post offices and newsstands. Public phones are rapidly disappearing with the advent of cheap mobile-phone calls and Skype.

➡ You must always dial 06 when ringing mobile phones, which have specific area codes depending on the company.

➡ Consider buying a rechargeable SIM chip, which will reduce the cost of making local calls.

Tourist Information

Budapest Info (☏1-438 8080; www.budapestinfo.hu) has three branches in central Budapest and info desks in the arrivals sections of Ferenc Liszt International Airport's Terminals 2A and 2B.

Main branch (Map p66; V Sütő utca 2; ☺8am-8pm; Ⓜ M1/M2/M3 Deák Ferenc tér) Best single source of information about Budapest.

Castle Hill branch (I Szentháromság tér 6; ☺9am-7pm Apr-Oct, to 6pm Nov-Mar; 🚌16) Small and often very busy in summer.

Oktogon branch (Map p98; VI Liszt Ferenc tér 11; ☺10am-6pm Mon-Fri; Ⓜ M1 Oktogon, 🚌4, 6) Least busy branch.

Travellers with Disabilities

Budapest has made great progress in recent years with making public areas and facilities more accessible to travellers with disabilities. Wheelchair ramps, toilets fitted for those with disabilities, and inward-opening doors, though not as common as in Western Europe, do exist and audible traffic signals for the vision impaired are becoming commonplace, as are Braille plates in public lifts.

Visas

EU and Schengen countries No visas required.

Australia, Canada, Israel, Japan, New Zealand and USA No visa required for stays of up to 90 days.

Other countries Check the website of the **Hungarian Foreign Ministry Consular Service** (http://konzuliszolgalat. kormany.hu/en).

Language

Hungarian is a member of the Finno-Ugric language family; it is related very distantly to Finnish and Estonian. There are approximately 14.5 million speakers of Hungarian.

Hungarian has polite and informal forms; when addressing people you don't know well, use the polite form. In this language guide, polite forms are used.

To enhance your trip with a phrasebook, visit **lonelyplanet.com**.

Basics

Hello. (singular/plural)
Szervusz.   ser·vus
Szervusztok.   ser·vus·tawk

Goodbye.
Viszont-   vi·sawnt·
látásra.   laa·taash·ro.

Yes./No.
Igen./Nem.   i·gen/nem

Please. (pol/inf)
Kérem.   kay·rem

Thank you.
Köszönöm.   keu·seu·neum

You're welcome.
Szívesen.   see·ve·shen

Excuse me.
Elnézést   el·nay·zaysht
kérek.   kay·rek

Sorry.
Sajnálom.   shoy·naa·lawm

How are you?
Hogy van   hawd' von

Fine. And you?
Jól. És Ön?   yāwl aysh eun

Do you speak English?
Beszél angolul?   be·sayl on·gaw·lul

I don't understand.
Nem értem.   nem ayr·tem

Eating & Drinking

The menu, please.
Az étlapot,   az ayt·lo·pawt
kérem.   kay·rem

I'd like a local speciality.
Valamilyen helyi   vo·lo·mi·yen he·yi
specialitást   shpe·tsi·o·li·taasht
szeretnék.   se·ret·nayk

What would you recommend?
Mit ajánlana?   mit o·yaan·lo·no

Do you have vegetarian food?
Vannak önöknél   von·nok
vegetáriánus   eu·neuk·nayl
ételek?   ve·ge·taa·ri·aa·nush ay·te·lek

I'd like..., please.
Legyen szíves,   le·dyen see·vesh
hozzon egy...   hawz·zawn ej...

Cheers! (to one person)
Egészségére!   e·gays·shay·gay·re

Cheers! (to more than one person)
Egészségükre!   e·gays·shay·gewk·re

That was delicious!
Ez nagyon   ez no·dyawn
finom volt!   fi·nawm vawlt

Please bring the bill.
Kérem, hozza a   kay·rem hawz·zo o
számlát.   saam·laat

Shopping

I want to buy ...
Szeretnék venni ...   se·ret·nayk ven·ni ...

I'm just looking.
Csak nézegetek.   chok nay·ze·ge·tek

Can I look at it?
Megnézhetem?　meg·nayz·he·tem

How much is this?
Mennyibe kerül　men'·yi·be ke·rewl
ez?　ez

That's too expensive.
Ez túl drága.　ez tūl draa·go

There's a mistake in the bill.
Valami hiba van a　vo·lo·mi hi·bo von o
számlában.　saam·laa·bon

Emergencies

Help!
Segítség!　she·geet·shayg

Go away!
Menjen el!　men·yen el

Call the police!
Hívja a　heev·yo o
rendőrséget!　rend·ēūr·shay·get

Call a doctor!
Hívjon　heev·yawn
orvost!　awr·vawsht

I'm lost.
Eltévedtem.　el·tay·ved·tem

I'm sick.
Rosszul vagyok.　raws·sul vo·dyawk

Where are the toilets?
Hol a véce?　hawl o vay·tse

Time & Numbers

What time is it?
Hány óra?　haan' āw·ra

It's (one/10) o'clock.
(Egy/Tíz) óra van.　(ed'/teez) āw·ra von

morning	*reggel*	reg·gel
afternoon	*délután*	dayl·u·taan
evening	*este*	esh·te
yesterday	*tegnap*	teg·nop
today	*ma*	mo
tomorrow	*holnap*	hawl·nop

1	*egy*	ed'
2	*kettő*	ket·tēū
3	*három*	haa·rawm
4	*négy*	nayd'
5	*öt*	eut
6	*hat*	hot
7	*hét*	hayt
8	*nyolc*	nyawlts
9	*kilenc*	ki·lents
10	*tíz*	teez
100	*száz*	saaz
1000	*ezer*	e·zer

Transport & Directions

Where's (the market)?
Hol van (a piac)?　hawl von (o pi·ots)

What's the address?
Mi a cím?　mi o tseem

Can you show me (on the map)?
Meg tudja　meg tud·yo
mutatni　mu·tot·ni
nekem (a　ne·kem (o
térképen)?　tayr·kay·pen)

Does it stop at (Parliament)?
Megáll　meg·aall
(Parlamenthez)　(por·lo·ment·hez)
on?　on

What time does it leave?
Mikor indul?　mi·kawr in·dul

Please stop here.
Kérem, álljon　kay·rem aall·yawn
meg itt.　meg itt

Is this taxi available?
Szabad ez a taxi?　so·bod ez o tok·si

Behind the Scenes

Send Us Your Feedback

We love to hear from travellers – your comments help make our books better. We read every word, and we guarantee that your feedback goes straight to the authors. Visit **lonelyplanet.com/contact** to submit your updates and suggestions.

Note: We may edit, reproduce and incorporate your comments in Lonely Planet products such as guidebooks, websites and digital products, so let us know if you don't want your comments reproduced or your name acknowledged. For a copy of our privacy policy visit lonelyplanet.com/privacy.

Steve's Thanks

I'd like to thank friends Bea Szirti, Balázs Váradi, Erik D'Amato, Tal Lev and Ildikó Nagy Moran for helpful suggestions, assistance and/or hospitality on the ground. Péter Lengyel showed me the correct wine roads, and Michael Buurman opened up his flat, conveniently located next to the Great Synagogue. I'd like to dedicate this book to my partner, Michael Rothschild, with love and gratitude.

Acknowledgments

Cover photograph: Hungarian Parliament, Doug Pearson/Alamy.

This Book

This 1st edition of Lonely Planet's *Pocket Budapest* was researched and written by Steve Fallon, and produced by the following:

Destination Editor Brana Vladisavljevic **Product Editors** Elin Berglund, Katie O'Connell **Senior Cartographer** Valentina Kremenchutskaya **Book Designer** Jessica Rose **Assisting Editors** Sarah Bailey, Melanie Dankel, Andi Jones, Kate Mathews **Assisting Book Designer** Clara Monitto **Cover Researcher** Naomi Parker **Thanks to** Daniel Corbett, Karyn Noble, Sally Schafer, Dianne Schallmeiner, Tony Wheeler

Index

See also separate subindexes for:

⊗ Eating p156

☺ Drinking p157

✪ Entertainment p157

🔒 Shopping p157

Our Writer

Steve Fallon

Steve, who has worked on every edition of Lonely Planet's *Budapest* guide, first visited Hungary in the early 1980s by chance – he'd stopped off on his way to Poland (which was then under martial law) to buy bananas for his friends' children. It was a brief visit but he immediately fell in love with thermal baths, Tokaj wine and *bableves* (bean soup). Not content with the occasional fleeting fix, Steve moved to Budapest in 1992, where he could enjoy all three in abundance. Now based in London, he returns to Hungary regularly for all these things and more: *pálinka*, art nouveau, the haunting voice of Marta Sebestyén, and the best nightlife in central Europe.

Published by Lonely Planet Publications Pty Ltd
ABN 36 005 607 983
1st edition – June 2015
ISBN 978 1 7436 0513 4
© Lonely Planet 2015   Photographs © as indicated 2015
10 9 8 7 6 5 4 3 2 1
Printed in China